Y0-ABU-559

SISTER TO SISTER

OTHER BOOKS AND AUDIO BOOKS
BY MARILYNNE TODD LINFORD:

Sisters in Zion

We are Sisters

SISTER TO SISTER

Marilynne Todd Linford

Covenant Communications, Inc.

Covenant®

Cover image *Comforting* © Anita Robbins

Cover design copyrighted 2009 by Covenant Communications, Inc.

Published by Covenant Communications, Inc.
American Fork, Utah

Copyright © 2009 by Marilynne Todd Linford
All rights reserved. No part of this book may be reproduced in any format or in any medium without the written permission of the publisher, Covenant Communications, Inc., P.O. Box 416, American Fork, UT 84003. This work is not an official publication of The Church of Jesus Christ of Latter-day Saints. The views expressed within this work are the sole responsibility of the author and do not necessarily reflect the position of The Church of Jesus Christ of Latter-day Saints, Covenant Communications, Inc., or any other entity.

Printed in Canada
First Printing: March 2009

16 15 14 13 12 11 10 09   10 9 8 7 6 5 4 3 2 1

ISBN-13: 978-1-59811-818-6
ISBN-10: 1-59811-818-8

With love and confidence in the next generation,
this book is dedicated to

Michael
Caitlin
Jason
Jared
Sarah
Alex
Joshua
Mariah
John
Abby
Rachel
Jenna
Adam
Rebecca
Benjamin
Nathan
Jacob
Eric
Andrew
Brooke
Amelia

TABLE OF CONTENTS

Preface and Acknowledgments 1

In-law Relationships Matter 3

The Four Worst Things Good Wives Do 9

The Parenting Pyramid 13

The Seven Worst Things Good Parents Do 17

How Important Is a Mother's Prayer? 21

Applying Lessons from "Mothers Who Know" 25

21 Ideas to Help Raise a Boy 29

12 Ideas to Help Raise a Girl 35

Teaching Children about Marriage 41

Teaching Children about Civility 45

Teaching Children to Love Their Country 49

Teaching Children about the Sacrament 53

Teaching Children about the Millennium 57

"My Cup Runneth Over with Love" 61

Does the Lord Know Your Name? 65

Will the Lord Strengthen You? 69

Giving Gives Back 73

Hope for a Better World 77

The Gorilla Detector 81

Antidotes and Alternatives to Worry 85

Recognizing Tender Mercies..89

"The Wind Did Continually Blow" 93

Stuck in Time, or The Case for Continuing Revelation 97

Accelerating Harvest Time 99

An Eyewitness into the Hereafter 103

"What Goes on Inside Your LDS Temples?" 107

The Great Leveler and Elevator 111

Life Is for Giving 113

A Gift That Keeps on Giving 117

Where and When Did Joseph Smith Learn Chiasmus? 121

Sister Scriptorians and Hidden Treasure 125

The High Price of Irreverence 129

Do You Have Pioneer Courage? 131

That's What I Get Paid the Big Bucks to Do 135

You Are Invited 139

Sabbath Keepers 143

A Parable: "Ye Took Me In" 147

Why Only a Few Are Chosen 151

War's Lessons 155

The Case for No Left Turns 159

How to Move Mountains 161

The Face of a Saint 163

The "Crucialness" of Crucial Conversations 167

Expect a Miracle Soon 171

Tools 175

Index 179

PREFACE AND ACKNOWLEDGMENTS

Every month for the past nine years, I've written a one-page message for the sisters of my ward. It's been an unofficial calling from my Relief Society presidents—Sue Smith, Carol Pia, Carole Kirk, and Kristine Philips. I've enjoyed writing these messages and have written with a prayer that the words would be beneficial to some sister in the ward. When Covenant Communications saw a broader purpose and wider audience for the messages, I prayed to know your needs. Several times, as new topics came to mind, thoughts flowed so simply it was as though I was an observer watching the words appear on the computer screen without forethought or plan. All the so-so work is mine; everything filled with the Spirit came by the Spirit.

After *Sisters in Zion* came *We Are Sisters.* At a book signing a woman came up to me and said, "I know the name of your next book in the Sister series."

"There's going to be another book?" I asked.

"Yes," she said, "and it's titled *Sister to Sister.*" I hadn't thought about a Sister series, and I wish I had asked this woman her name. If you are this sister, please let me know who you are. I'd like to give you a hug and thank you in person.

This is another book of short chapters, averaging about one thousand words each—the length of my attention span. I hope you'll like the variety. All are for women—some specifically for young women, some for mothers, and some for women who are waiting for their husbands and children to show up. Some are ideas for family home evenings, some I hope men will read, some are for fun, but all in all, I hope something will have been written that gives you a spiritual boost.

I thank my mother for the ability she has to give spiritual boosts. I'm thankful for her incredible stability and love and for my father's tenacity to principle. I'm thankful to them for giving me seven siblings. As the oldest of that tribe and mother of eight of my own, I've had the opportunity to quasi- or actually parent fifteen children. And, as expected, just when I think I've finally got something right, a new challenge appears. I'm grateful for my husband, who willingly edits everything I write. How I appreciate his love and testimony. I'm grateful for our children and grandchildren, for their love and strength and for the good times we have together. I love my daughters-in-law and sons-in-law who hopefully don't have a laundry list of scary mother-in-law stories about things I have or haven't done. I'm thankful for my sisters who are dearest friends and for my friends who are like dear sisters. My brothers are a source of wisdom and good humor. I am also thankful to my gospel sisters with whom I share or have shared callings.

I extend specific thanks and appreciation to my editor, friend, and daughter, Elizabeth Lehnhof, who skillfully and unrelentingly identified the so-so portions of the book and made them less so-so. She is nice and kind and tough as nails. I also thank my Covenant editor, Eliza Nevin, who used her refining skills to put the finishing touches on the manuscript.

I know the doctrines discussed in these pages are true. I pray for you and for me—that we will faithfully and courageously travel this adventure in womanhood, motherhood, and sisterhood at this complex and historic time called the latter days.

IN-LAW RELATIONSHIPS MATTER

When two women from different family cultures and different generations love the same man, one as his mother and one as his wife, and are linked by law—not by their choosing—in a relationship with each other because of him, there are going to be "issues." These issues, however, must be addressed, especially in a gospel context, where the Lord expects us to live a higher law. The tenet "Thou shalt live together in love" (D&C 42:45) does not mean that you are expected to love your mother-in-law or daughter-in-law only if you are living under the same roof. Whether you live together or thousands of miles away from one another, it is a commandment to communicate with and act toward each other with love. A second scripture commands, "Thou shalt love thy neighbour as thyself" (Matthew 22:39). So how do mothers-in-law and daughters-in-law "live together in love" and love each other as neighbors?

Stories about the disagreeable mother-in-law (MIL) are popular subjects for jokes. Unfortunately, there truly are some mothers-in-law who have been unneighborly, unfriendly, unkind, and unloving. For example (these are all true): Cynthia's MIL sent her a letter listing all the things she should change about herself to better fit in with the family. When Tammy's MIL came for a visit, she rearranged every cupboard in the kitchen because "it was all wrong." Maria's MIL also came for a visit. After being shown where she would sleep and the bathroom she would use, she said, "Why did you give me blue towels? Don't you know guest towels are supposed to be white?" Marta's MIL always comes with gifts for the oldest and youngest children but never for the one in the middle. Becky's MIL shows a preference for the grandchildren who look like her side of the family. Shelly's MIL sent her to the store to buy a long list of groceries and gave her a credit card to pay for it. The credit card was maxed out. Shelly never mentioned it and paid for the groceries herself. She didn't think much about it until it happened again. Pat's MIL paid for her grandchildren to fly to her home to stay for a week, then sent them home a day early in their pajamas. Linda's MIL mutters comments such as, "I've never seen anybody in all my days do it like that, but if you choose to do it that way, well, I guess that's your business." Suzanne's MIL warned her son not to marry Suzanne because she plays the violin. Debbie's MIL refused to accept the fact that Debbie and her son were married. She called Debbie's husband every night at ten and insisted on talking to him for an hour.

There are also plenty of stories about the not-so-nice things daughters-in-law have done to their mothers-in-law, but since the mother-in-law is older, should be more mature, has more life experience, has complete control over her own actions, and has probably been a daughter-in-law herself and seen firsthand the good and bad from that viewpoint, the mother-in-law has the greater responsibility. In fact, let's assign the mother-in-law 100 percent of the responsibility for the relationship.

"But, but, but," you mothers-in-law are saying. "That doesn't sound fair. What do I do about my daughter-in-law who is so close to her own mother that there is no room in her heart for me?" Another says, "What do I do? My daughter-in-law seems jealous of me and keeps me from seeing my son and grandchildren." "What do I do?" frets another mother-in-law. "My daughter-in-law refuses to come to family functions."

The daughter-in-law does have some accountability for the relationship—the Lord commands it. He said, "Honour thy father and thy mother" (Exodus 20:12), which includes parents-by-marriage. This commandment comes before "do not kill" and "do not commit adultery," which shows us that honoring parents is very important to the Lord. So, daughters-in-law, honor your mothers-in-law. As for assigning responsibility, since the daughter-in-law is usually younger, she can more easily adapt to new situations and personalities. Since she has had fewer of life's experiences, she should learn from those who have traveled the road before her. Since she also has complete control over her own actions, and since she owes her mother-in-law thanks for rearing her husband, what would you think about making the daughter-in-law responsible for 100 percent of the relationship?

"But, but, but," you daughters-in-law are saying. "What do I do if I have one of the controlling, self-centered mothers-in-law described above? What if I've done everything I know how to do to be respectful to her and she continues to treat me with disrespect? What if she takes no responsibility and makes no effort to have a relationship with me?"

Of course, there is no single solution to every in-law situation, but the basics can help. The first thing to do is to pray for yourself in your role as a daughter-in-law or mother-in-law. Pray that you will see the situation as it really is and not as anger, pride, or insecurity dictate. Pray to repent of whatever degree of self-importance is keeping you from loving as our Savior commands. Pray for patience and to see her good qualities.

Next, pray for her. Pray that she will know of your desire to "live together [with her] in love." Pray that her heart will be softened toward you, that she will realize your good intent, and that she will understand that you want your relationship with her to be mutually beneficial.

In conjunction with these prayers, guard your tongue. Don't say anything you wouldn't want said to or about you. Be mindful of the way you look at her. Make sure you have gentleness in your eyes and be alert, as occasion permits, to ways you can serve her, not doing what *you* would want but what *she* wants. Learn her favorites and ask her to show you how she does things. Learn from each other, serve each other, expect and accept differences, speak kindly to and of each other, compliment and complement each other, never complain about the other to anyone, be sensitive to each other's needs, share experiences, accentuate the things you have in common, write, call, give gifts to each other, celebrate each other's special days, and work and play side-by-side. In most cases, the years will melt away any arrogance and vanity and there will be a mutual affection—maybe never perfect, but good enough.

Daughters-in-law, a very compelling reason for you to establish a good relationship with your mothers-in-law is that your children are listening, watching, and learning about in-law relationships. One day you will be the mother-in-law to their spouses.

In real life, some incompatibilities never resolve themselves, but hopefully, they can be shoved in a corner so you can coexist peacefully. There may be other situations where the best solution is to live as far away from each other as possible. Rarely, a worst-case circumstance arises wherein either the mother-in-law or the daughter-in-law is such a negative, potentially dangerous, or evil influence that the relationship must be severed to protect the marriage and/or the children. But this conclusion must usually be the decision of the spouse, not the in-law. In the majority of situations, however, time, prayer, and love can overcome most obstacles, because you never know when you, either as a daughter-in-law or as a mother-in-law, will become essential to the other.

Michelle is a mother of six and a stake Primary president. Lani is the stake Primary secretary, a mother of six, and grandmother of ten. Recently Michelle and Lani exchanged e-mails.

Subject: Baby not here yet.

Michelle, my daughter-in-law Emily has not delivered and is in tears about the thought of my leaving and not being here to take care of Willis while she is in labor. She is scheduled for an induction Thursday because there are no available hospital beds before then. In planning my trip we did not consider the possibility that this baby would be late, because Willis arrived right on time. What are your feelings about my staying here longer? It would mean I would not be there for the stake Primary activity day. I do have the cookies, frosting, charms, and bags all ready to go, but that means only three of you. YIKES. Lani.

Subject: RE: Baby not here yet.

Lani, I have some very good news that should make you feel a lot better. The stake presidency is calling a new stake Primary board member tonight, and I've been planning on inviting her to help with the activity. Also, we have invited the ward activity day leaders to come and help. Of course, you will be missed, but we will be fine. Just let me know how I can get the items you have prepared.

So you know how I truly feel about this situation, I would do the activity alone, if I needed to, so you could stay with your daughter-in-law. I have some experience here. The day my first child was born, everything appeared fine. My parents soon left, but my mother-in-law felt impressed to stay with me. Because she was there, my husband felt comfortable returning to work. Within a few hours, my mother-in-law alerted a nurse that I wasn't acting like myself. And then, when no action was taken, she made her voice heard. I was subsequently rushed to the ICU with a life-threatening infection, and my husband and parents were summoned to my bedside to say good-bye. I do not remember this. I have only been told about her insistence and determination. I will always be grateful for the fact that my mother-in-law stayed with me.

Oh, Lani, there is no comparison in the world of the importance of the activity day to the birth of Emily's baby. Stay and enjoy the precious moments and days, and give her the security and comfort of your presence and help. You're where you're supposed to be. Don't let any worry about the activity distract you from the wonderful service you are providing. Michelle.

Michelle is my daughter. You can imagine the feelings I have for her mother-in-law who stayed with her while I went on my merry way, thinking everything was fine. At a minimum, I owe her thanks for every minute since then that Michelle and I have had to enjoy each other as mother and daughter and for the five additional grandchildren that have come.

Staying power seems to be a singular trait of daughters- and mothers-by-marriage as they respond to each other's needs. If you ever find yourself on either side of this equation and need extra strength, remember the example of

Michelle and her mother-in-law, and stay there. Remember the example of Lani and her daughter-in-law, and stay there. Remember how, in the Old Testament, Ruth, the daughter-in-law, and Naomi, the mother-in-law, supported each other and stayed with each other, giving us the most beautiful words a daughter-in-law could say to her mother-in-law: "And Ruth said [to Naomi], Intreat me not to leave thee, or to return from following after thee: for whither thou goest, I will go; and where thou lodgest, I will lodge: thy people shall be my people, and thy God my God: Where thou diest, will I die, and there will I be buried: the LORD do so to me, and more also, if ought but death part thee and me" (Ruth 1:16–17). In-law relationships matter and can be this beautiful.

THE FOUR WORST THINGS
GOOD WIVES DO

I'm not an expert, but I have discovered by experience, observation, and trial and error four of the worst things good wives do. The first of the worst is what I'll call, "Oh, it's okay, my wife always fixes it" syndrome. One Saturday James told his eleven-year-old son Kevin that as soon as his room was clean, they would go on a hike. Kevin ran to his room and was back in seconds. James put his arm around Kevin's shoulder and said he wanted to see a room that could be cleaned that quickly. As James surveyed the bed covers sloppily pulled up, the pillows helter-skelter, clothes draped over the back of a chair and on the desk, and books lying here and there, he said, "This room is not clean." Kevin retorted, "Oh, it's okay, Mom always fixes it." When Kevin's mother heard that she always "fixes it," things began to change. In psychological jargon it would probably be called *enabling*. When we do for others what they should do for themselves, we enable them to shirk their responsibilities. This deprives them of skill improvement and the satisfaction that comes with a job well done.

The marital symptoms of the "fix it" syndrome mirror Kevin's ingratitude and expectation of more. I always and forever want to be helpful and show the scriptural "lovingkindness" (Psalms 92:2) to my husband, but I don't want to be the cause of my own problems. No one appreciates a doormat. I asked a few friends if they were also guilty of the "fix it" syndrome. One told me about the day she was exasperated because her husband said he would mow the lawn when he got home from work on Friday, but several Fridays passed by and the grass was ankle high. Finally she couldn't stand it and decided to mow it herself before he got home. She got the mower out and was trying to start it when he came home. He said, "I'd advise you not to mow the lawn."

"Why not?" she said.

"You do it once and it will become your job forever."

She didn't mow the lawn.

Another friend told me about making sack lunches for everyone, including her husband. Quite often one of the children or her husband would complain about something in or not in the lunch. One day it occurred to her that it really wasn't her job. Each was perfectly capable of making his or her own lunch. When she quit the lunch-making business, her family realized how much they missed the service and begged her to be their lunch lady again, promising they'd never, ever complain. With a smile, she just shook her head.

Another friend told me she often used the phrase "Thanks for helping me with my work" when a family member helped her with household duties. Then one day she was struck by an epiphany: "It's not *my* work. Housework is everyone's work."

In the same way, I've found that if I take over a responsibility that is really Richard's, he lets me keep doing it, not because he's lazy or thoughtless, but mostly because the things I do seem to just magically happen and don't come to his awareness. To misquote D&C 121:39, "I have learned by sad experience that it is the nature and disposition of almost all men (and children), as soon as their wives (or mothers) perform a task they should perform for themselves, they will immediately begin to exercise unrighteous dominion (expecting more without reciprocating or showing appreciation)."

The solution to this problem is usually quite simple. Identify an area in which you are the fixer, stop doing whatever it is, and watch what happens. There will be some adjustment time, but while the dust is settling, be pleasant yet consistently firm. Then, after the new way of doing things is definitely in place, move on to the second item on your list. Your husband and children will gain skills, feel a sense of accomplishment, and respect you.

The second worst thing good wives do is think their husbands can read their minds. You know how it happens; you've experienced it a million times. It plays out when you want to go to your parents' home for Thanksgiving because your sister who lives in Alaska is going to be there, but in the every-other-year rotation you've traditionally followed, it's your turn to be at your in-laws'. So you subtly tell your husband about this wonderful trip your sister has planned. You bring up the fact that Thanksgiving is coming. You hint at how long it's been since you've had any time with your sister. You tell him little incidents from your childhood to show how close you and your sister were. Then your mother-in-law calls and gives your husband a food assignment for Thanksgiving dinner. When you realize he has accepted a food assignment, you fall into deep despair because he isn't meeting your needs, or being under-standing, or compassionate, and so on. After you spend a couple of days moping around like a sick cat, he recognizes the pattern and asks you what you are upset about. The truth is you didn't communicate with him about what you wanted. You expected him to be clairvoyant. The solution is a direct and unemotional conversation in which you come right out and present the dilemma and ask him how you can spend time with your family while not neglecting his. Listen to how he feels. Usually, there is more than one way to solve a problem that can meet his needs as well as your own. Men solve problems. If they know what their wives want and don't feel manipulated, they are usually willing to help.

The third worst thing good wives do is to be critical, which is negative, uncaring, unloving, prideful, and the gateway to contention, besides being wrong. King Benjamin said, "And ye will not have a mind to injure one another, but to live peaceably. . . . And ye will not . . . fight and quarrel . . . with [your husband], and serve the devil, who is the master of sin, or who is the evil spirit which hath been spoken of by our fathers, he being an enemy to all righteousness" (Mosiah 4:13–14; I hope King Benjamin is okay with my additions and deletions).

We are women, and we want things done the way we like them done, according to our timetable. So when something isn't happening exactly in the moment or order or method we expect or like, we tend to find fault with our husbands, who may actually be attempting to help. Usually it's not about right and wrong; it's about style. It's like the difference between priesthood quorum meetings and Relief Society. Somehow the gospel still gets taught without a tablecloth, fresh flowers, a handout, a special musical number, and a treat. Men are men, and they see the world differently, which is why marriage is between a man and a woman. Some problems are solved better by men, some by women, and usually the best solution is discovered when the couple works together rather than being critical of each other's methodology, trying to do it alone, or criticizing the other into capitulation. Criticism doesn't motivate; it discourages.

The best way to resolve differences is to find a humorous approach. A wonderful stake patriarch said it this way: "After sixty years of marriage we still have our differences. My wife lives by the maxim, 'If a job's worth doing, it's worth doing well.' I say that while that may be true, it doesn't account for the fact that perhaps the job didn't need to be done in the first place." There are good ways to get things done—not your way or my way, but our way. Instead of finding fault, use kindness and gratitude, two of the best motivators and builders of healthy relationships. I'm speaking to myself: Listen to your husband, take his righteous counsel, express gratitude to him, don't criticize him, work as a team, and know that no man is going to do things exactly like a woman.

Which segues into the fourth worst thing good wives do, which involves another area of communication. Basically, we talk too much. Women like to rehash and delve and probe and think out loud. Women especially like to rehash and delve and probe and wonder out loud about the past. Sometimes we just can't let the past be in the past. Women tend to verbally analyze everything, from why soap scum is forming in the shower to why fifteen years ago on Christmas Eve he said. . . .

Talking through problems, deciding a course of action together, and sharing thoughts and feelings are all good within reason. But too often we think we have to say everything we think. We don't. We need to put a filter on our brains to catch idle, foolish, and hurtful thoughts before they hit the tongue. As we well know, once something is verbalized, it can't be retracted. I find I talk most when I'm nervous and talk least when I'm sad. When one of our sons was dating, he said his dates would hardly talk at all until he took them to get something to eat. He said as soon as food began to fill their stomachs, it was like flipping a talking switch. Whatever it is that triggers the need to share, it's important in all relationships to listen at least as much as you talk. John Adams, the second president of the United States, said that George Washington had "the gift of silence, [which] . . . I esteem as one of the most precious talents" (David McCullough, *John Adams* [New York: Simon & Schuster, 2001], 593). Knowing when to be silent is a gift worth cultivating.

Happy marriages are a work in progress. I'm trying to talk less about things that don't matter and more about those that do instead of expecting him to read my mind. I'm trying to listen more and curb my tendency to be critical. I pray that I won't try to fix everything and that I'll have the wisdom to know what I should do for him, what he should do for me, what he should do for himself, and what I should do for myself, and I pray I'll be patient and more patient and more and more patient with the process. Perhaps that's why we believe in marriage for eternity—it will take me that long to get it right!

THE PARENTING PYRAMID

You are familiar with the food pyramid established in 1992 by the United States Department of Agriculture (USDA) as a guide for healthy eating. This food pyramid advised us to eat six to eleven servings of grains; three to five servings of vegetables; two to four servings of fruits; two to three servings of meat, poultry, fish, beans, eggs, nuts, and seeds; and two to three servings of milk, cheese, yogurt, or milk substitutes each day. At the top of the triangle were listed the foods to be eaten only occasionally—fats, oils, and sweets. In 2005, this pyramid was updated, but the amount of fats, oils, and sweets is still the smallest fraction by far. (You might like to take a look at this new eating guide at http://mypyramid.gov.) If you are like many Americans, you eat way too much of the fats, oils, and sweets. Many of us eat proportions exactly opposite of what the USDA recommends. Even though we know that eating according to these guidelines will make us healthier, most of us have difficulty applying the principles.

The idea of using a triangle to illustrate important principles has also been used in teaching parents about specific activities that will increase family unity. Dr. Brian J. Hill, a Brigham Young University professor of recreation management, asserts that family unity has three facets: cohesion (how close family members feel to each other), adaptability and flexibility (how readily and appropriately family members adjust to change and adversity), and communication (how effectively family members exchange ideas with one another). His interest in how recreational activities can improve family unity came as he studied "The Family: A Proclamation to the World," which lists "wholesome recreational activities" as the last of nine ways to strengthen families.

Through time diaries, Dr. Hill has been able to show how individuals spend their 168 hours each week, minute by minute. Each day the average person spends:

Twenty minutes with the whole family, typically eating dinner together

About two hours with part of the family, most often when a parent is driving children to lessons or practices

Each week, the average person spends:
Forty hours at work
Twenty-two hours in family care, shopping, preparing meals, doing laundry, and doing house and yard work
Seventy-two hours in personal maintenance, including sleep
Forty-one hours of discretionary time

Dr. Hill's purpose is to teach parents the importance of using more of the forty-one unallocated hours for joint family activities. He stresses that family activities don't just happen. There are too many forces out there in the world pulling families apart. He also believes that family activities must be purposeful, which means they take planning and effort. In this family recreation pyramid, he illustrates the types and frequency of the activities that strengthen families:

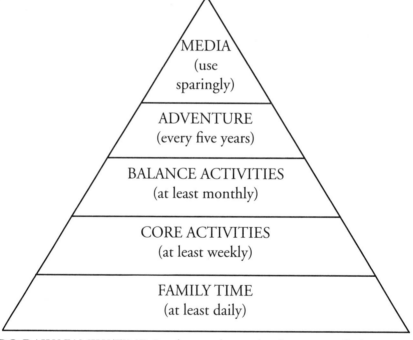

MEDIA
(use sparingly)

ADVENTURE
(every five years)

BALANCE ACTIVITIES
(at least monthly)

CORE ACTIVITIES
(at least weekly)

FAMILY TIME
(at least daily)

DO DAILY FAMILY TIME. Just be together under the same roof—home, car, sky—at the same time.

DO WEEKLY CORE ACTIVITIES such as enjoying family dinners, singing together, playing board games, baking cookies, doing crafts, gardening, playing catch, attending a child's soccer game, going to church activities.

DO MONTHLY BALANCE ACTIVITIES such as eating out, ice skating, camping, boating, going to the theater or zoo, and taking vacations. (A vacation by definition must span at least one night.)

DO ADVENTURES ABOUT EVERY FIVE YEARS. Adventures are major family events that are too costly in time, energy, and resources to happen very often. The best adventures are not leisure and luxury activities, but rather are challenging—even hard.

USE MEDIA SPARINGLY. Using the media for family time is the least productive activity. Media is usually an individual experience rather than a family one because there is limited interaction.

Like the food pyramid, the family recreation pyramid gives sound advice. But just as the food pyramid can't guarantee the health of an individual, the family recreation pyramid can't guarantee the health of a family. Why? Because we don't take counsel well. Just as with sweets and fats, most of us use media in reverse proportion to the foundations, or basics, of the pyramids—grains and family time.

Dr. Hill sums up with a plea: "Do stuff together. Do more stuff together. . . . Don't be afraid to do hard stuff!" (Brian Hill, "Strengthening Families through Wholesome Recreation," BYU Education Week, 16 Aug. 2004; this talk can be viewed at www.byutv.com.)

THE SEVEN WORST THINGS GOOD PARENTS DO

I was lost in thought, scanning the endless rows of books in a bookstore, when a title made me feel panicky even as I reached for it. Of all the things I want and strive to be in life, even slightly more than being a good wife—now there's a confession for you—I want to be a good parent. And here was a book that could prove I had committed one or two, perhaps even all seven, of parenting's deadly sins. I felt condemned as I opened *The 7 Worst Things Good Parents Do,* by John C. and Linda D. Friel (Deerfield Beach, Florida: Health Communications, Inc., 1999), and turned to the table of contents. Guilt blurred my vision, but I was finally able to focus on the number-one worst thing: "Baby your child."

For starters, and this isn't an excuse, I wasn't prepared for motherhood. When our firstborn came, I was only twenty-two. How was I supposed to know when I shouldn't treat him like a baby anymore? Well, yes, you do remember correctly; I am the oldest of eight children, but being the oldest sibling did not quite prepare me for becoming a mother. I can remember looking heavenward and wondering how Heavenly Father could trust me with one of His precious children. By the time I had kind of, sort of, figured it out, there were seven more children, and I was dropping our firstborn off for his first day of junior high school. I drove him; I didn't let him walk with his friends. Guilty on the first count.

My eyes moved to number two of the worst things good parents do. I read, "Put your marriage last." Holy smoke! You just read my confession. There were days, many of them, when I never surfaced from mothering long enough to recall how it was that I got all those children. Richard, poor Richard, blessed Richard. Fortunately, it was also his desire to have many children. In fact, on our first date, he told me he wanted me to be the mother of his children. It's true. So I thought about it and decided the only decent thing I could do was to marry him before we started that process. And the heavens smiled upon us, granting us our desire for a large family. If you asked him if there were times he felt neglected, he'd smile and say, "There might have been a few." Guilty on count two.

Inhaling, I looked at number three of the worst things good parents do: "Push your child into too many activities." Of course, anything times eight is too many everythings, but I did try to help the children maximize and realize their talents. (Likely the justification every over-programming parent uses.) At one point we had three pianos to accommodate all the practicing. I'd move from piano to piano helping each child, hoping they'd soon be motivated enough to practice by themselves. Often I'd have a baby on my hip as I counted, "One and two and three and four and." When our sixth child went to kindergarten and starting learning to count, her teacher reported that she counted, "One and two and three and four and . . ." There were piano lessons for everyone, flute for one, trumpet for two, voice for several, baseball, football, basketball, volleyball, track, and soccer in too many seasons and uniforms to count. And ballet. How I love ballet, and all four girls got the chance to dance. Count three: guilty as charged.

With one eye closed, I looked at the next of the seven worst things: "Ignore your emotional or spiritual life." This may be directed to the parent guilty of ignoring his or her own emotional or spiritual life, but it brought to mind how I had failed in remembering that of my children. Oh, how many mistakes I had made in disregarding the subtleties of each child's emotional and spiritual needs. I immediately recalled the day Anne, Elizabeth, and Christine were playing with the new dolls they had received for Christmas. As I went from girl to girl to braid their hair, I was happily enjoying their interaction, feeling good about the give-and-take among them. At some point I realized there were two new big beautiful dolls and one kind of shabby little doll. "Where's the other big doll?" I asked. Instantly, two pairs of eyes stared incredulously at me, while the third pair filled with tears. She said, "I don't have a big doll. You forgot to buy me one." I was sure I'd scarred her for life. Just one example of too, too many times I'd ignored one my children's emotional and spiritual well-being. I felt convicted on count four.

By now, I was quite sure I'd committed all seven unpardonable parenting sins. Number five read, "Be your child's best friend." I immediately remembered the day I went to my parents' home with the good news that I had been hired as an English teacher at a nearby junior high school. My parents expressed happiness at the adventure before me—four classes of seventh-grade English and two of eighth-grade English for a total of two hundred and twenty-two students! My father, who was a high school principal, said, "Almost all first-time teachers make the same mistake. Don't try to be your students' friend. Don't smile 'til after Christmas." Well, I smiled at them on the first day of school, and that's just how I parented. I like being liked. Add another guilty ruling.

I looked at the next parenting sin. Number six read, "Fail to give your child structure." I felt like giving a little cheer. I'm a list-maker and love to organize things and people. I began to reminisce about summers at our house when the children were young. We had devotionals and charts with stickers and reading time and field trips and bedtime rituals. I felt I could honestly say, "Not guilty. My children had structure."

I looked at the last item in the list of the worst things good parents do. It stated, "Expect your child to fulfill *your* dreams." Well, you just read that I love ballet, so my daughters took ballet; I love playing the piano, and all eight took piano lessons. I wonder, though, if that is enough to convict me. I don't know. How passionate do you have to be about having your children do what you love to turn a good thing into a negative for the child?

After this self-analysis, I had some interesting afterthoughts. For example, the principle "Don't baby your child" could be written as the opposite: "Don't neglect your child." A middle-of-the-road suggestion would say, "Help your child mature and learn life skills as she moves through developmental stages. If you shelter and protect her from learning to take a shower by herself because she might slip and fall or get burned, you are babying her. If you never keep track whether she showers and don't teach her how to shampoo her hair, you are neglecting her." It suddenly became clear that good parenting means staying away from extremes. If you put your weight to either side of the parenting balance beam, you'll fall off. Good parenting avoids the edges. Too little is neglect; too much smothers. The other worst things good parents do that are on the Friels' list all have their opposites, which are just as "worst."

"Don't put your marriage last" is a good maxim, but don't put your children last either. Life isn't either/or. Why should I have to put one of my two most important callings in life last? What if I'd gone overboard by being the best, most perfect wife, but let our children raise themselves? The truth is I can't be a good wife if I neglect my children, and I can't be a good mother if I neglect their father. Both marriage and mothering responsibilities must be woven together to knit a strong family. Marriage does come first, but children are a very close second.

"Don't push your child into too many activities" is wise, but don't let them spend their waking hours playing video games or running unsupervised in the neighborhood or at the mall. And the truth is, most every child needs to have a little encouragement or "pushing" to complete their daily tasks.

"Don't ignore emotional and spiritual life," of course, is very important for children as well as parents, but don't be the kind of parent who intrudes too much. You don't have to take their emotional and spiritual temperatures every day. Fluctuations are normal and children need some privacy. Give them enough legroom to learn to use their agency and to become safely independent.

"Don't fail to give your child structure" is a middle-of-the-road statement somewhere between letting the neighbors raise your children and programming every minute of their lives. I don't know how the Friels would feel about the amount of structure in my home. As with everything else in parenting, some of my children would probably say I was too structured, some not enough, and, hopefully, a few would say I was right on.

"Don't expect your child to fulfill your dreams" probably has to do with the degree of interference from the parent. Forcing a child into a sport or hobby or career is wrong, but so is not having dreams for your child. I hope I responded to my children's dreams, helping each identify strengths and talents, and then at an appropriate point, stepped back and let them fulfill their own dreams.

It was a productive exercise for me to evaluate myself by the Friels' standards, and they give some concrete and thoughtful ideas. I looked at the title of the book again and realized their "worst" list is actually a pat on the back. The book is about *good* parents. You are a good parent as you evaluate your performance and keep trying to be better. You are a good parent as you love your children and work to improve your parent-child relationships. You are a good parent when your efforts are to help your children grow up to be happy, productive adults who will one day also strive to be good parents.

HOW IMPORTANT IS A MOTHER'S PRAYER?

David (names have been changed) rented a room in an older home near BYU. Five other returned missionaries were also renting in the house. After the first week of class he changed his schedule and came home from campus at a time he was not expected. David's housemate Henry seemed to be home as well because David could hear him talking through the wall. He listened to see if he could figure out who was with Henry, but he could only hear Henry's voice. Finally, David's curiosity got the best of him, and he stepped into the hall to look into Henry's room. Through the door, which was just slightly ajar, David saw Henry on his knees, praying aloud to his Father in Heaven. Worried that he might have interrupted, he quickly returned to his own room.

A while later, the talking stopped, and David went into Henry's room to apologize. Soon, their conversation turned to the topic of vocal prayers. Henry explained that one day, when he was reading Joseph Smith's History, verse 14 made him stop and think. Joseph wrote, "It was the first time in my life that I had made such an attempt, for amidst all my anxieties I had never as yet made the attempt *to pray vocally*." Henry felt prompted to try vocalizing his own prayers and, like Joseph, "retired to the place where [he] had previously designed to go, having looked around [him], and finding [him]self alone, [he] kneeled down and began to offer up the desires of [his] heart to God" (Joseph Smith—History 1:14–15; emphasis added). Unexpectedly, he found that when he followed the Prophet Joseph Smith's example of *speaking* his prayers rather than just *thinking* them, Heavenly Father seemed nearer, and the act of praying became more sacred and more intense. But it was hard to find private times and places to pray aloud until he realized that he could juggle his class schedule to find a time when his roommates were in class and he could be alone. David, in turn, felt prompted to follow the example of Henry, who was following that of Joseph Smith. Have you ever wondered if Joseph was following anyone's example?

In the *History of Joseph Smith by His Mother,* Lucy Mack Smith writes that she "became deeply impressed with the subject of religion" and desired that her husband share her interest. When Joseph Sr.'s brother, Jesse, belittled this desire, Joseph Sr. pulled back. Lucy became concerned and decided to make it a matter of prayer. She said, "I retired to a grove *not far distant,* where I prayed to the Lord in behalf of my husband" (ed. Preston Nibley [Salt Lake City, UT: Bookcraft, Inc., 1956], 43; emphasis added). Joseph Smith's mother prayed in a grove probably very similar to another grove future generations would call sacred. She established a pattern. Upon reading James's instruction, "If any of you lack wisdom, let him ask of God" (James 1:5), Joseph chose a grove not far from his home and received the divine answer in response to "the boy's first uttered prayer" ("Joseph Smith's First Prayer," *Hymns,* no. 26).

However, Mother Smith's influence on her son was not limited to the location of his first vocalized prayer. More importantly, Joseph learned the power of prayer at his mother's knee. Regarding her prayer for her husband, she wrote, "After praying some time in this manner, I returned to the house much depressed in spirit, which state of feeling continued until I retired to my bed. I soon fell asleep and had the following dream." She tells of seeing a meadow with two very beautiful, very tall trees. "I saw one of them was surrounded with a bright belt, that shone like burnished gold, but far more brilliantly." This tree was "encircled with this golden zone" and seemed "most lively and [animate]. . . . If it had been an intelligent creature, it could not have conveyed, by the power of language, the idea of joy and gratitude so perfectly as it did." When she looked at the other tree, it didn't have any light but stood "fixed as a pillar of marble. No matter how strong the wind blew over it, not a leaf was stirred, not a bough was bent; but obstinately stiff it stood." As she wondered what it meant, she received the interpretation: The trees represented her husband and his brother. "The stubborn and unyielding tree was like Jesse; that the other, more pliant and flexible, was like Joseph, my husband; that the breath of heaven, which passed over them, was the pure and undefiled gospel of the Son of God, which gospel Jesse would always resist, but which Joseph, when he was more advanced in life, would hear and receive with his whole heart, and rejoice therein" (*History of Joseph Smith by His Mother,* 43–45).

No doubt Joseph had heard his mother rehearse this wondrous, comforting event, including the location of her prayer. It's likely that since his mother had received a vision following her prayer, Joseph's faith was that he, too, could receive a direct answer to his petition. The Apostle James had written, "But let him ask in faith, nothing wavering" (James 1:6). Perhaps his mother's experience allowed Joseph to ask in unwavering faith. We can also assume that Lucy prayed more than once in the grove and about many, many of the concerns she had in her life.

Samuel, Lucy's fourth son and Joseph's younger brother, was also taught by his mother to value and utilize the power of prayer:

He possessed a religious turn of mind, and at an early age joined the Presbyterian Church, to which sect he belonged until he visited his brother Joseph in Pennsylvania in May 1829, when Joseph informed him that the Lord was about to commence his latter-day work. He also showed him that part of the Book of Mormon which he had translated, and labored to persuade him concerning the gospel of Jesus Christ, which was about to be revealed in its fulness.

Samuel was not, however, very easily persuaded of these things, but after much inquiry and explanation he retired and prayed that he might obtain from the Lord wisdom to enable him to judge for himself; the result was that he obtained revelation for himself sufficient to convince him of the truth of the testimony of his brother Joseph.

[On] May 15, 1829, Joseph Smith and Oliver Cowdery were baptized, and as they were returning from the river to the house, they overheard Samuel engaged in secret prayer. Joseph said that he considered that a sufficient testimony of his being a fit subject for baptism; and as they had now received authority to baptize, they spoke to Samuel upon the subject, and he went straightway to the water with them, and was baptized by Oliver Cowdery, he being the third person baptized in the last dispensation. (*History of Joseph Smith by His Mother*, 337)

Another son following his mother's example.

I too have been blessed by my mother's righteous example of prayer. I remember walking past her room on bright, sunny days and catching a glimpse of her kneeling by her bed. Seeing her bathed in sunlight conversing with her Heavenly Father is a digital-quality image burned forever in my mind. However, my photo-like memory of form and light is insignificant compared to the lifelong desire her example instilled in me to communicate with my Heavenly Father. I hope that I too can be an example to my children and grandchildren as they see and hear me pray.

APPLYING LESSONS FROM "MOTHERS WHO KNOW"

Sister Julie B. Beck, Relief Society general president, began her talk in October 2007 general conference by retelling the Book of Mormon story of the two thousand courageous young warriors who were men of truth because they had been taught by their mothers "to walk uprightly before [God]" (Alma 53:21). These faithful young men paid tribute to the faith their mothers had taught them, saying, "We do not doubt our mothers knew it" (Alma 56:48). Sister Beck spoke to the mothers of today, challenging them to be "mothers who know."

The ripple effects of this talk were many and marvelous, as mothers throughout the Church reassessed their priorities. One mother, when asked to describe the feelings she had during Sister Beck's talk, said, "I was thankful for the choices I've made. I especially liked her comment, 'There is power in motherhood.'"

Sister Beck challenged mothers to turn their homes into pre-missionary training centers. She instructed mothers to teach the doctrines of the gospel in family scripture study, family prayer, family home evening, and at mealtimes, so that when their son or daughter arrived at the MTC, the doctrines would "be a review and not a revelation."

After hearing this talk, a mother of three elementary-age children made each a missionary name tag and instituted what she calls "pre-mission preparation." This is how PMP works in their home: About once a week, the children are told to put on their missionary name tags and report to a certain room in the house. There, their mother instructs them in a missionary skill such as sewing on a button, or making macaroni and cheese, or reading and discussing a topic from *Preach My Gospel.*

Several mothers, responding to questions about the talk's effect, mentioned that the topic about "mothers who do less" really got their attention. Financially, they don't have to be as frugal as their mothers and for sure not as frugal as their grandmothers. And they live in a culture that seems to advocate that more and bigger is always better. But Sister Beck said, "Mothers who know do less." What do they do less of? Anything that "will not bear good fruit eternally. . . . Less media . . . less distraction, less activity that draws their children away from their home. [They] . . . live on less and consume less of the world's goods." Why? "In order to spend more time with their children." "Doing what?" you might ask. Spending "more time eating together, more time working together, more time reading together, more time talking, laughing, singing, and exemplifying."

Sister Beck summed up the underlying principle of mothers who do less to do more: "Their goal is to prepare a rising generation of children who will take the gospel of Jesus Christ into the entire world. Their goal is to prepare future fathers and mothers who will be builders of the Lord's kingdom for the next fifty years. That is influence; that is power."

A divorced sister who has no children felt comforted by Sister Beck's words, "Faithful daughters of God desire children." She found specific direction as the word *nurturing* penetrated her heart. Sister Beck reminded her that she doesn't need to be a mother to nurture the rising generation. This sister happens to be an early-morning seminary teacher, and after this talk, she began thinking of the students in her class more as her children. She had a picture taken of the students standing around her and printed it on her Christmas card. The text read, "From my early-morning family to your family."

Sister Beck gave *nurturing* an expanded definition, saying, "Another word for *nurturing* is *homemaking*. Homemaking includes cooking, washing clothes and dishes, and keeping an orderly home. . . . Growth happens best in a 'house of order,' and women should pattern their homes after the Lord's house (see D&C 109). Nurturing requires organization, patience, love, and work. Helping growth occur through nurturing is truly a powerful and influential role bestowed on women."

A mother of six took Sister Beck's closing statement personally. This mother explained that she had always considered herself the intellectual type and never thought of homemaking skills as important. "In fact," she confessed, "I dislike housework, and my home shows that I'd rather be doing anything than keeping my house neat and tidy." When Sister Beck said, "women should pattern their homes after the Lord's house," an idea this mother had heard many times before, she agreed in principle but considered "a house of order" ideal but impossible with her skills and interests. However, when Sister Beck closed her talk by saying, "I have every confidence that our women will do this," she was struck to her core. In relating what happened she said, "Sister Beck said she has confidence in me. That means I can do it."

The next day after the school children were gone and the baby was asleep, she took a tour of her home to find a place to start. She looked at her bedroom and was embarrassed at what she saw through her new eyes. It was not "a house of order." She said she actually blurted out, "Why, I haven't even been a good roommate to my husband." Immediately, she began to organize and clean their bedroom. Is her home suddenly neat and tidy? "It will always be a struggle," she adds, "but Sister Beck has faith in me. She thinks I can do it, so I'll keep trying."

There *is* power in motherhood. Thanks, Sister Beck, for your counsel and confidence. (See Julie B. Beck, "Mothers Who Know," *Ensign,* Nov. 2007, 76–78.)

21 IDEAS TO HELP RAISE A BOY

The three most important principles in rearing girls and boys are the same:

1. Teach each child that he or she is a child of God, that God loves him or her, and that each can speak to Him in prayer.
2. Show each child that you love him. Mister Rogers said it best: "I love you just the way you are."
3. Know that your child has come preprogrammed to pass through specific developmental stages and that most behavioral issues are tied to this fact. The trick is to know when a behavior is outside the normal range. On pages 110 through 116 of *Teaching, No Greater Call: A Resource Guide for Gospel Teaching* (1999), there is a basic list of age group characteristics.

It is commonly found, however, that boys are loud, active, physical, and competitive. Boys often mature, gain small motor control, and differentiate between reality and fantasy later than girls. Boys are many times more likely to be diagnosed with hyperactive disorder and much more likely to get in trouble. The average boy is less social, less verbal, and has a shorter attention span than the average girl. To further complicate the complex, many girls are the object of some boys' aggressive behavior at one point or another. When these girls become the mothers of boys, they may prevent normal, active play, fearing it will evolve into the aggressive behavior they themselves experienced. The consequence is that some boys grow up being punished for being male. Aggressive play can hurt, bully, or intimidate—all of which are inappropriate. But normal, active play is energetic, imaginative, creative, and usually very loud. Boys pretend they are superheroes saving humanity. They pretend they are firemen, policemen, and paramedics saving the neighborhood. They roughhouse and wrestle, and, if supervised and taught properly, their play can be wholesome and devoid of aggression. So how do you harness the energy?

Provide Role Models

The most significant help a mother has in raising a son is his father. "Boys want to grow up to be like their fathers. . . . Every boy loves his father and wants to be able to do what he does, both to honor him, to earn his praise, and to compete with him. . . . Boys who grow up in homes with absent fathers search the hardest to figure out what it means to be male. . . . Men are extremely important in giving boys messages about being a man" (Geoffrey and Michael Thompson, in "The Search for Masculinity: Growing Up Masculine," www.pbs.org/parents/raisingboys/masculinity02.html). If there is no father in the home for a son to pattern after, his mother must find another man who can somewhat fill this void. The boy's maternal grandfather is the next best choice, if he is a positive influence. Mothers without husbands should be wary of trusting their boyfriends to fill this role. As boyfriends can come and go, the child could become ever more confused about manhood.

Set Limits

When parents set appropriate limits, the world is more predictable and safer. With no limits, a boy will test and push against unspoken limits. When there are no limits, discipline never makes sense. Parenting is not a popularity contest, so if your son crosses a limit or line, no matter how he protests, the planned consequence or punishment must be enforced.

Exercise Prevention

Keep weapons, power tools, matches, medicines, and all potentially dangerous items locked up. The best-equipped ambulances in the valley can never make up for the missing guardrail at the top of the hill.

Take Action

If the boy's play is hurting someone, you must immediately remove him from the situation to protect the other child or children. There are two responses parents may implement. Sometimes a timeout where the boy must sit quietly works. Other times, a timeout where physical energy is mandatory is a better alternative. One family disciplined their aggressive seven-year-old when he was jumping over his baby brother from bean bag chair to bean bag chair in ever-increasing distances by making him run up and down the fourteen steps in their home ten times. When the child finally tired, his mother demonstrated with a stuffed animal to show the boy how potentially dangerous his jumping was. Too many mothers yell from the other room or momentarily interrupt a telephone call to try to stop the behavior. When action is required, take action.

Address Fear

Fears are common in all children, but boys are often taught not to express them. They are conditioned to think they must be big and brave. When a mother encourages a son to come to her with questions or worries and treats his inquiries and feelings with respect, his trust in her increases. She can assure him that even grownups have anxieties and that there are healthy ways to handle his fears. Unresolved fears often lead to acting out.

Watch for Acting Out

Some boys act out or copy the behaviors they see in the media. Monitor and limit the video games he plays or watches others play. Monitor and limit the television shows and movies he watches. Talk to him about what is real and what is fantasy. Talk to him about how it feels to be a victim. Help him begin to develop empathy. Give him physical play options to use up aggressive energy such as throwing and catching a ball, kicking a ball into a net, running, skipping, jumping, or racing. Boys like to build and take things apart, so help them learn to use tools (not anything sharp or electric, and, of course, always with close supervision).

Use Zero Tolerance

Set absolute limits on physically hurting another. There is no excuse and should be no tolerance for hitting, biting, or pushing of any kind. Also— and this is so important—your boy must be taught that play of any kind must stop when another child feels distressed or says, "Stop," especially when the other child is female. Boys need to have that same control over their own bodies. When an overly friendly, seemingly innocent grand- parent, aunt, uncle, or neighbor tickles the child, the child does not have to endure it. If he tells the tickler to stop, the parent must make sure the tick- ling or any other behavior that makes the child uncomfortable stops. This is true for parents as well. The Church, and for the most part, society, has zero tolerance for physical, sexual, or emotional abuse of any kind.

Provide Physical Work

Give him age-appropriate physical work. The joy of a job well done builds self-esteem and competence. Working alongside his father or grandfather offers him perspective of a man's role in the family and the world. Chores should be required, whether picking up toys, feeding the dog, or helping to clean up after dinner. Reward him with specific praise for a job well done: "Your closet looks great. I like the way you lined up your shoes."

Use Reading

In quiet times, read him true stories of boys and men who made life better for others. Find his areas of interest and read books about those interests—animals, doctors, veterinarians, construction workers, athletes, etc. Do what it takes—your time and, if necessary, after-school tutoring—to make sure your son is a good enough reader. Many problems can be averted when a boy has the confidence of being a good reader. When a boy sees his parents read for recreation, especially his father, he will more likely enjoy reading. You can read aloud to boys until they leave home for college or a mission. Boys who have been read to will read by themselves and to others. "You may have tangible wealth untold; / Caskets of jewels and coffers of gold. / Richer than I you can never be — / I had a Mother who read to me" (Strickland Gillilan, "The Reading Mother").

Encourage Writing

Writing is also very important. Help boys learn to form letters correctly and to write legibly. You learn to write by writing, just as you learn to ride a bike by riding. Helping him record the events of his life in a journal encourages writing. This creates a priceless history and is good practice. Journal entries don't have to be long. A young boy could draw a picture and valiantly try to print his name. It's the effort and experience that count.

Encourage Verbal Expression

Increase his verbal skills by listening to him as he relates the events of his day. Encouraging conversation with eye contact, appropriate verbal signs, and body language shows that you are paying attention. Interjections of "Oh," "Uh-huh," and "How interesting" from you will lengthen the story, and the experience will improve his storytelling skills.

Don't Say "Don't" So Often

Record the number of times you say "don't" in a day. You may be surprised. Try to be more positive.

Remember That Hovering Is for Hummingbirds, Not Mothers

Only children and youngest and oldest children are the most likely to have hovering mothers. Don't be a hummingbird or a micromanager. If you are an overly attentive mother, back away gradually and give him the space he needs to gain the independence he will need in the future.

Catch Him Being Good

Praise his good qualities publicly, accurately, and in his presence. Compliment him in front of his father, grandparents, friends, and neighbors. They will pick up the cue and also encourage him. Keep his faults an in-house issue between you and him.

Provide Choice

Give your boy an opportunity to make choices. It can be as simple as letting him choose the color of his shirt or the flavor of his ice cream. Gradually give him more and more control over his life, preparing him to gain the skills needed to live on his own.

Allow No Choice When Appropriate

Children should not be given the opportunity to choose when they don't have the maturity to make a right choice. There is no choice whether or not to eat vegetables, but the choice can be broccoli or carrots. There is no choice about going to church, but he can choose what color of socks to wear.

Never Control with Emotional Abuse

A boy learns to emotionally abuse others as he observes his parents manipulating his environment under the guise of teaching a lesson. A child should never be coerced or controlled by adult whims, by anger, by passive-aggressive behavior, by threat of physical violence, or by withdrawal of necessities or affection.

Provide Order

Boys need order. Have a time to get up and a time to go to bed, a time to eat, work, and play. Include him in planning the day, but don't be too rigid. Moments of spontaneity, like a hug for no reason or going on an unplanned walk, brighten routine.

Teach Emotional Courage

Teach boys that masculine strength includes faith, humility, and empathy. Teach them that real life is where real courage occurs. This will help counter the media's suggestions that being macho and defeating a larger opponent denotes courage. Help your son see true manhood in the man who goes to work every day to support his family, in the father who forgoes a professional sporting event to watch his child in a school play, or in the husband who helps his wife in the ways she needs.

Discipline to Build Character

Help your son know that everyone gets into trouble and that consequences always follow poor choices. Discipline logically and consistently, never harshly or in anger or to shame. "The best discipline is built on the child's love for adults and his wish to please. If that impulse is respected and cultivated, children will continue to be psychologically accessible through their love and respect. If they are unduly shamed, harshly punished, or encounter excessive adult anger, they will soon react to authority with resistance rather than with a desire to do better" (Dan Kindlon and Michael Thompson, "Nurturing and Protecting the Emotional Life of the Boy in Your Life as detailed in *Raising Cain*," http://www.powderhouse.net/downloads/RaisingCain7points.pdf).

Relax

Much of the behavior in young boys that concerns mothers is developmental. It will disappear with maturity. The almost incessant activity, exploration, curiosity, and enthusiasm are functions of maturation. They are expressions of the lack of experience seeking experience. Pray for the Lord's help. Listen for promptings from the Holy Ghost. Remember that most mothers are good enough for most children. You don't have to be perfect, Mom. You are doing great. Have fun, love him, and show it!

12 IDEAS TO HELP
RAISE A GIRL

The three most important principles in raising girls are the same as those for raising boys:

1. Teach each child that he or she is a child of God, that God loves him or her, and that each can speak to Him in prayer.
2. Show each child that you love her. Mister Rogers said it best: "I love you just the way you are."
3. Know that your child has come preprogrammed to pass through specific developmental stages and that most behavioral issues are tied to this fact. The trick is to know when a behavior is outside the normal range. On pages 110 through 116 of *Teaching, No Greater Call: A Resource Guide for Gospel Teaching* (1999), there is a basic list of age group characteristics.

Commonly, girls are gentler, quieter, and less physically aggressive than boys. You don't often see a little girl run at full speed across a room to tackle another girl. Girls often mature, gain small-motor control, and differentiate between reality and fantasy earlier than boys. Girls are less likely to be diagnosed with hyperactive disorder and less likely to get in trouble. The average girl is more social, more verbal, and has a longer attention span than the average boy.

As you look back on your girlhood, hopefully you have pleasant memories of afternoon lemonade parties with teddy bears, jumping rope until your sides and legs ached, reading under a shady tree, dressing up for a special occasion, climbing trees, or playing baseball. And you have a great, obvious advantage in knowing how to raise a girl because you are one. (If you are wondering why there are 12 ideas for raising a girl and 21 ideas for raising a boy, I don't know, either. I just wrote until it felt done.)

Enjoy Being Female

You are your daughter's role model of how to be a wife, mother, daughter, sister, daughter-in-law, aunt, friend, and woman. You model priorities and balance as you juggle daily demands on your time and energy. You model emotional health as you demonstrate good ways to handle stress and what to do when you are sad, sick, or angry. Your attitude and actions reveal the value you give marriage and motherhood and whether they are worthwhile goals. Your life is your testimony of being female. Your life is your definition of womanhood.

Marry a Man Who Will Be a Good Father

The very best thing you can do for your daughter is to marry a man who will be a good husband and father, and stay married to him. President James E. Faust quoted Karl Zinsmeister in "Fathers, Mothers, Marriage" (*Ensign*, Aug. 2004, 2): "The father's influence increases as the child grows older. . . . 'It's well established that the masculinity of sons and the femininity of daughters are each greater when fathers are active in family life.'" Elder Richard G. Scott counseled fathers, "Be a wise father who showers attention on each daughter. It will bring joy to you and fulfillment to her. When a daughter feels the warmth and approval of her father, she will not likely seek attention in inappropriate ways. As a father, acknowledge her good behavior. Listen to her and praise her for her strengths. You will greatly enrich her life. She will model the behavior she observes. Let her see you treat your wife and other women with admiration and honest respect" ("The Sanctity of Womanhood," *Ensign*, May 2000, 36). Help your husband meet these expectations.

Be Unified as Parents

Let your daughter know from her earliest understanding that Daddy and Mommy are a team, traveling life's seas together, sitting in the same boat, rowing in the same direction. Again from Karl Zinsmeister: "There is a large measure of complementarity in male and female parenting. The demands on fathers and mothers shift back and forth as a child passes through different developmental stages. There is no question that men and women tend to provide children with different things, in different ways. . . . A child who is highly involved with both parents has the full spectrum of response from which to learn" (*Fathers, Who Needs Them?* [address delivered to the Family Research Council, 19 June 1992]). "The Family: A Proclamation to the World" defines these distinct yet complimentary roles: "By divine design, fathers are to preside over their families in love and righteousness and are responsible to provide the necessities of life and protection for their families. Mothers are primarily responsible for the nurture of their children. In these sacred responsibilities, fathers and mothers are obligated to help one another as equal partners" (*Ensign,* Nov. 1995, 102).

Mold Character

Instill in your daughter the belief that nothing trumps integrity. Teach her to seek after the virtuous, lovely, and good things of the world. Teach her to be refined in speech and action. Let her see that you live what you teach, that there is no hypocrisy in you. Help her to develop strength, wisdom, and courage.

Emphasize Education

From the day of her birth teach your daughter to prize learning. You've heard, "When you educate a girl, you educate a nation." Help her want to know facts, gain knowledge, and understand how things work. Help her to develop study skills. Help her want to do her best. Help her to achieve to her ability level and beyond. Emphasize that education combines native intelligence and hard work and that, of the two, hard work most often takes you farther.

De-emphasize Appearance

From her earliest years, counter societal pressures with their corrupt messages about body image. Model modesty and femininity. Teach her that Heavenly Father designed and created males and females for divine purposes. Avoid dressing her like a teen when she's three, and don't make name-brand clothing important. As you help her establish healthy eating and exercise habits, don't compare her body shape and size to anyone else's. As you well know, many of the complex aspects about physical size are part of our DNA package and cannot be changed, but sometimes parents may need to intervene in tactful, extra-loving ways. Teach her that pretty is as pretty does. Teach grooming skills and manners. Teach her that the purpose of looking nice is to give her confidence, so she can concentrate on what the teacher is saying or what is needed instead of being preoccupied about how she looks. Help her accentuate her best physical features, which, for many girls, is her smile. If she feels self-conscious about smiling because her teeth are crooked, do what it takes to get them straightened. The more she uses her smile, the happier her life will be. Also, if her complexion isn't clear, help her learn how to care for her face. Brigham Young said, "Beauty must be sought in the expression of the countenance, combined with neatness and cleanliness and graceful manners" (*Discourses of Brigham Young,* ed. John A. Widtsoe [Salt Lake City, UT: Deseret Book Company, 1954], 214).

Guide Her to Autonomy

Girls who have a sense of self-sufficiency and confidence can better withstand the pressure to do another's bidding or to give in when they should say no. Girls who don't respect themselves are vulnerable in every aspect of life. In the article, "Helping Teens Stay Strong," professors Brent L. Top and Bruce A. Chadwick wrote, "Generally speaking, those youth who avoided delinquency came from families where parents expressed appreciation and showed love; guided them through high expectations, family rules, and accountability; and allowed teens to have their own thoughts and opinions without resorting to intimidation, fear, guilt trips, or withholding love. . . . These characteristics relate to positive outcomes such as achieving social competence and emotional health—not just avoiding delinquency" (*Ensign,* Mar. 1999, 27).

Teach the Value of Money

Women run households. If they are not good money managers, they will struggle now and later. Brigham Young said, "When I go into a house, I can soon know whether the woman is an economical housekeeper or not; and if I stay a few days, I can tell whether a husband can get rich or not. If she is determined on her own course, and will waste and spoil the food entrusted to her, that man will always be poor. It is an old saying that a woman can throw out of the window with a spoon as fast as a man can throw into the door with a shovel; but a good housekeeper will be saving and economical and teach her children to be good housekeepers, and how to take care of everything that is put in their charge" (*Discourses of Brigham Young,* 213).

Strive for Emotional Stability

Women are often seen as more emotional, which is both good and bad. Good because we are more expressive and demonstrative; bad because we can have more ups and downs—hence the drama-queen jokes. However, the happiest girls and women are those who maintain a steady, positive, realistic approach with reason and common sense. Help girls learn how to discipline and control their mood swings.

Teach Good Communication Skills

Teach each girl to read, write, and spell as well as possible. Help her express herself with clarity. Start young by encouraging her to tell a story, share an experience, or explain an idea. Teach good listening skills by listening to her.

Value Her

As a girl becomes a teen, her level of self-worth may decrease—even plummet. Self-image stays more constant when a girl feels loved and supported by her family and when she has things she knows she does well. Wise parents know that self-confidence is based on fact. Use childhood to help your daughter develop skills and abilities by which she can define herself. Praise her efforts. And besides being good at certain things, she also needs to know she is good. Abraham Lincoln said, "When I do good, I feel good." Help her become involved in doing good by serving as age appropriate in the home, the ward, and the neighborhood, which helps her both feel good and do good.

Love Her

Do girl stuff together. Bake, shop, exercise, watch chick flicks, laugh, cry, share, hug. Talk. Listen. Listen. Talk. Listen. Listen. Don't try to be her best friend. Don't dress, talk, or act like her. She needs you to be her mother, not her peer. Help her develop skills for her future roles. Know she will make mistakes. You will make mistakes. Model saying, "I'm sorry." Pray with her and for her. Listen for and act on promptings from the Holy Ghost. Teach her, love her, and expect great things from her.

TEACHING CHILDREN
ABOUT MARRIAGE

Because the definition of marriage is now regularly making headlines, today's children need to be taught about marriage in ways former generations never thought were necessary. A family from California was staying with another family. At dinner one evening, the Californian five-year-old got the adults' attention when he stated, "Did you know that marriage is between a man and a woman?" Congratulations to the parents for teaching truth! It's not likely that the child was taught this definition of marriage in the public school system.

Teach your children the Biblical account of the first marriage on earth. "God created man in his own image . . . male and female created he them. And God blessed [married] them, and God said unto them, Be fruitful, and multiply, and replenish the earth, and subdue it" (Genesis 1:27–28). "And Adam called his wife's name Eve; because she was the mother of all living" (Genesis 3:20).

Teach your children the doctrine in "The Family: A Proclamation to the World," which states, "Marriage between a man and a woman is ordained of God and . . . the family is central to the Creator's plan. . . . All human beings—male and female—are created in the image of God. Each is a beloved spirit son or daughter of heavenly parents. . . . Gender is . . . [an] eternal identity. . . . In the premortal realm, spirit sons and daughters knew and worshiped God . . . and accepted His plan . . . of happiness. . . . Sacred ordinances and covenants . . . in holy temples make it possible for individuals to return to the presence of God and for families to be united eternally. . . . Happiness in family life is most likely to be achieved when founded upon the teachings of the Lord Jesus Christ. Successful marriages and families . . . [have] faith, prayer, repentance, forgiveness, respect, love, compassion, work, and wholesome recreational activities. . . . Fathers are to preside over . . . provide [for] . . . and [protect] . . . their families. Mothers are [to] nurture . . . their children" (*Ensign,* Nov. 1995, 102).

Teach your children the order of life. Wise use of the teenage years includes graduating from high school, defining and refining talents, and dating in groups. The early twenties are best spent beginning necessary training and education for a career, a mission (for eligible young men and, if desired, for eligible young women), more schooling as needed, marriage, beginning a family, and more school if desired. When life happens in this order, happiness and success are much more likely than when done in any other order. Statistics prove that marrying while a teen is a great risk. Eleanor H. Ayer writes in her book *Everything You Need to Know About Teen Marriage* that, "A girl married at 17 is twice as likely to be divorced as a girl 18 or 19. If a girl waits until she is 25 the chances that her marriage will last are 4 times better" (New York: The Rosen Publishing Group, Inc. [1991], quoted in "Relations and Marriage—Teen Marriage," 123HelpMe.com). On the opposite end, waiting to marry until every bit of possible education is completed unnecessarily postpones marriage and starting a family until the mid-thirties for some who seek advanced degrees.

Teach your children to counsel with their parents and Heavenly Father in selecting a mate.

Teach your children the importance of marrying the right person. The number-one suggestion in H. Jackson Brown, Jr.'s "21 Suggestions for Success" reads, "Marry the right person. This one decision will determine 90% of your happiness or misery" (www.21suggestions.com). President Gordon B. Hinckley said, "[Marriage] will be the most important decision of your life. . . . Marry the right person in the right place at the right time" ("Life's Obligations," *Ensign*, Feb. 1999, 2). "Marriage is perhaps the most vital of all the decisions and has the most far-reaching effects, for it has to do not only with immediate happiness, but also with eternal joys. It affects not only the two people involved, but also their families and particularly their children and their children's children down through the many generations" (Spencer W. Kimball, "Oneness in Marriage," *Ensign*, Mar. 1977, 3).

Teach your children the importance of temple marriage. "There is no substitute for marrying in the temple. It is the only place under the heavens where marriage can be solemnized for eternity. Don't cheat yourself. Don't cheat your companion. Don't shortchange your lives" (Gordon B. Hinckley, "Life's Obligations," *Ensign*, Feb. 1999, 2).

Teach your children that marriage requires effort. Don't teach them that marriage is easy and fun, but, on the other hand, don't make it sound too hard. Few marriages—mostly just those in fairy tales—are happily-ever-after experiences. Beginning in early childhood, teach your children relationship skills for coping with different personalities and conflict resolution techniques. Teach them empathy, how to understand another's feelings, and how to accommodate and work through the differences. Help children and teens learn to verbalize their own feelings and how they think others feel. Exemplify charity, longsuffering, and patience in adversity.

Teach your children how to preside, provide, protect, and nurture. As "The Family: A Proclamation to the World" states, these are their *primary* roles according to their respective genders. Of course, there is some overlapping needed to make marriage and family life work. But prophets of God—fifteen of them—have stated that fathers are to preside, provide, and protect. Mothers are to nurture. A good definition of *nurture* is to "train up a child in the way he should go" (Proverbs 22:6). "In these sacred responsibilities, fathers and mothers are obligated to help one another as equal partners" ("The Family: A Proclamation to the World").

Teach your children by example how to have a good marriage. Let them see that you take joy in the good things in your marriage. Tell them you believe that marriage is ordained of God. Wives, honor your husband's priesthood by helping him fulfill his priesthood duties at home and in the Church. Husbands, honor your wife's motherhood and support her in her callings at home and in the Church. As you both celebrate the good things about each other, you will teach the greatest lessons possible about marriage and family life. Then, when the inevitable conflicts come, show that solving problems in marriage is achieved by working through them, not by running away from them. Marriage is sacred and is the foundation for healthy families; families are the foundation for healthy nations.

TEACHING CHILDREN ABOUT CIVILITY

Civility is hard to define and, in real life, goes mostly unnoticed and unheralded. When a fellow driver hangs back so you can change lanes easily and safely, you acknowledge the kindness with a friendly wave of thanks. You may not spend the rest of the day telling everyone you meet about this moment in time, but it sets the tone for your day. With this positive experience, you are more inclined to reciprocate by responding to another fellow human being's need. Unfortunately, it is the situations where incivility is manifest that are noticed, discussed, remembered, and copied.

Civility occurs in the moment of decision and reveals your inner core. Do you love your neighbor as yourself? Do you believe one person can make the world a better place? Do you live the "Golden Rule," treating others as you would like to be treated? Are you kind, courteous, and polite? Do you show respect even when you are treated rudely? Can you put the stresses of your life aside and think of others' needs and wants? Civility is high-minded and self-sacrificing behavior. Civility is quiet and calm, patient and understanding. Civility is empathetically switching places momentarily, in your mind, with another human being and doing for him or her what you would want done to or for you if you were in his or her situation. Civility is positive interaction that shows respect for humankind. Civility is not just believing the golden rule, but living it.

It would be lovely if you could teach children about civility like your great-grandmother, who could show her humanity as she served a hot meal to a transient who was traveling across the country in a boxcar. Today, we've learned by tragic experience that you can't hire a homeless man to do work at your home as an evidence of your civility. Personal and family safety demands that we be cautious of people and situations. While children and teens should be taught civility, they must also be taught proper safety rules in every aspect of life. There are just too many bad people out there waiting to take advantage of the well-intentioned and innocent. So how can we teach our children to be cautiously civil?

Our local newspaper recently featured an article titled "Signs of the Times?" It wasn't about Biblical prophecy of wars and rumors of war. It was about civility, and the subtitle charged, "Civility May Be at All-time Low." The article reported on a poll listing ways society has become less civil. Heading up the list at number one was "language packed with enough four-letter words it would make people at your granddad's Navy reunion blush" (Dennis Romboy, "Signs of the Times? Civility May Be at All-time Low," *Deseret News*, May 11, 2008). Aha! There's a clue. Use clean language yourself and expect it of your children. There is no excuse, no reason, no occasion when foul language is needed. The poll showed a tie for numbers two and three—inappropriate use of cell phones and rude or reckless driving. We can teach teens disciplined cell phone use through role-playing various scenarios and by example. And reckless driving? Never! As you know too well, your example screams louder and longer than anything you try to say. How are your customer service and table manners? They also made the list. An interesting part of the poll showed that even though those polled felt that society as a whole has become less civil, most of the respondents felt their personal civility had stayed the same or improved. "People, in general, in surveys see the problem but very seldom do they see themselves as part of the problem," said P.M. Forni, who has written two books on civility and is director of the Civility Project at Johns Hopkins University (Romboy, 2008). We are all part of the problem.

As I read this article I wondered if being members of The Church of Jesus Christ of Latter-day Saints helps us be more civil. It should. A church named after the Savior, who is the Author of "Christian virtues," should be kinder, gentler, more sympathetic, and empathetic. We should be the most civil people on the planet because Jesus' teachings are all about civility: "Thou shalt love thy neighbour as thyself" (Matthew 19:19). "All things whatsoever ye would that men should do to you, do ye even so to them" (Matthew 7:12).

After I finished reading the *Deseret News* article, I remembered that before George Washington was sixteen, he "transcribed" a list of "Rules of Civility & Decent Behaviour in Company and Conversation." There are one hundred and ten of them, and they can easily be found on the Internet (see http://gwpapers.virginia.edu/documents/civility/transcript.html). They are completely delightful to read because many apply to a past generation. For example, number nine reads: "Spit not in the Fire, nor Stoop low before it neither Put your Hands into the Flames to warm them, nor Set your Feet upon the Fire especially if there be meat before it" (original spelling and punctuation retained). After you read these rules, you will probably groan and mutter something about how far we have strayed from this standard. You will wonder if there is a sixteen-year-old alive today who would not only copy such a list but also be concerned enough about civility to make it a part of his or her behavior.

A family home evening discussion of George Washington's transcription would be good for anyone. A reminder about table manners, about being polite, and about showing respect is always a good topic for family discussion. President Washington's number-one rule is: "Every Action done in Company, ought to be with Some Sign of Respect, to those that are Present." I love the positive way this rule describes civility. A sign of the times, the last sentence in the *Deseret News* article states the idea in a more crass way: "People who are nice . . . will in the long run have a network of [family and friends] who like and trust them. Who would choose jerk over good guy?" (Romboy, 2008).

Here are fourteen of George Washington's rules of civility, the first eleven (number nine is stated above) and the last four:

1st Every Action done in Company, ought to be with Some Sign of Respect, to those that are Present.

2d When in Company, put not your Hands to any Part of the Body, not usualy Discovered.

3d Shew Nothing to your Freind that may affright him.

4th In the Presence of Others Sing not to yourself with a humming Noise, nor Drum with your Fingers or Feet.

5th If You Cough, Sneeze, Sigh, or Yawn, do it not Loud but Privately; and Speak not in your Yawning, but put Your handkercheif or Hand before your face and turn aside.

6th Sleep not when others Speak, Sit not when others stand, Speak not when you Should hold your Peace, walk not on when others Stop.

7th Put not off your Cloths in the presence of Others, nor go out your Chamber half Drest.

8th At Play and at Fire its Good manners to Give Place to the last Commer, and affect not to Speak Louder than Ordinary.

10th When you Sit down, Keep your Feet firm and Even, without putting one on the other or Crossing them.

11th Shift not yourself in the Sight of others nor Gnaw your nails.

107th If others talk at Table be attentive but talk not with Meat in your Mouth.

108th When you Speak of God or his Atributes, let it be Seriously & wt. Reverence. Honour & Obey your Natural Parents altho they be Poor.

109th Let your Recreations be Manfull not Sinfull.

110th Labour to keep alive in your Breast that Little Spark of Celestial fire Called Conscience.

TEACHING CHILDREN TO LOVE THEIR COUNTRY

Unlike addition and subtraction, there is no test to measure a child's patriotism, because it isn't something of the mind; it's something in the heart. Even though it may be difficult to determine a child's level of patriotism, there are important reasons why parents should try to increase their child's love for his or her country. Learning about the great men and women who built their nation can give children a sense of who they are and who they can become. Studying their nation's history can give them a sense of belonging as they feel connected to something big and important. Understanding their country's past can influence their choices in the future and strengthen their resolve not to repeat history's mistakes. Loving their country can produce a desire to be an informed voter, to be involved in their communities, and even to run for public office.

Analyzing how I became patriotic has led me to conclude that each of us has our own testimony, so to speak, about this land. My husband's uncle, Chester Boss, loved to tell the story of how his father, Peter Boss, my children's great-grandfather, became a citizen. With tears in his eyes, he described what it was like to help his father study for the exam and the great anticipation and pride he felt the day his father, dressed in Sunday best, walked to the court-house to become a citizen of the United States. The details and tears revealed Uncle Chester's and Great-Grandfather's patriotism and boosted mine. I hope my children keep this and other precious stories like it alive so that future generations will remember their ancestors' sacrifices and great love for this country.

At the end of World War II, I was born in an army hospital on Governors Island in the shadow of the Statue of Liberty. Just a few weeks later, my father was deployed to the Philippine Islands. My father loved this country and felt honored to fight for its freedom. After the war he stayed in the army reserves until he retired. As a child, I loved to see him in uniform as he went to camp every summer, and I often went with him to do his work on Saturdays at Fort Douglas. In every prayer I ever heard him say, he thanked Heavenly Father for this free land and prayed for her leaders. He retired a full colonel. A few years before his death, when my out-of-state grandchildren were visiting my parents, a grandson asked if my father still had his uniform. Eighty-five years old, my father left the room and returned wearing his uniform. I hope my grandchildren remember seeing their great-grandfather standing straight and tall, proud to wear the uniform of the United States of America.

When my father died in 2004, a graveside honor guard fired a three-volley salute and "Taps" was played. An American flag draping his coffin was folded with great dignity and given to my mother. But the most touching moment occurred in the morning, when we pulled up to the ward building for the funeral. The bishop, a man who grew up in my home ward, a man who had had my father as his bishop, a man who knew my father's history, had lined the street in front of the church with large American flags. It was a fitting tribute from a man who personally understood my father's dedication to this country. I hope my children remember their grandfather's love for his country.

In 1971, my husband's employer transferred him to England, where we lived for three years. We traveled extensively to Scotland and Wales, Bath, Plymouth, Manchester, Brighton, Preston, Ipswich, Avon, and many other towns and villages. London was only twenty-three miles away, and we visited there often. We had a jolly good time. At the end of the three years, I loved the country of Great Britain. As we were leaving England, I wrote in my journal, "I know why they call Great Britain great. It is a great country." However, as we were in the plane getting closer and closer to New York City—my birthplace— my heart was pounding out of my chest. When we landed and were going through customs, I handed my passport to the officer at the port of New York. He was ready to send me through but paused to glance at my passport to see how long I'd been gone. Looking at me warmly he said, "Welcome home." How good it felt to be back in my native land. I cried. I hope I've shared my love for this country with my children.

The divine purpose of the United States is integrally linked to the Restoration of the gospel. The fertile soil of this "nation under God" is evidenced in the Book of Mormon. In 1 Nephi 13:10–19 we learn that God inspired Christopher Columbus to set sail to the west, that the Pilgrims would arrive, and that the settlers would fight a war to gain independence. It's amazing and wonderful that the Revolutionary War was seen in vision two thousand years before it happened! This is a land of promise. "Behold, this is a choice land, and whatsoever nation shall possess it shall be free from bondage, and from captivity, and from all other nations under heaven, if they will but serve the God of the land, who is Jesus Christ" (Ether 2:12). "God Bless America" is not a cliché. As a nation, we need the God of this land. I hope my children feel this truth.

As prophets have admonished us to have a photo or painting of a temple hanging in our homes, it seems prudent to also have something patriotic in our homes. It seems wise to take our children to patriotic events and to pray for our country and her leaders. Family home evenings can be used to teach about the Founding Fathers or about the first American in your family. You could read or even memorize the opening paragraphs of the Declaration of Independence, the Constitution, the Bill of Rights, or the Gettysburg Address and sing, listen to, or play patriotic songs together. You can travel to historic sites, and protect the environment. You can become involved in the political process and show your enthusiasm for particular candidates before the election and then lend support for those who win after the election, teaching your children that your love for this country remains constant as candidates come and go. You can honor and obey the laws of the land, fly the flag, sustain the armed forces, and show respect for local law enforcement. Teach your children that if freedom is lost, it is costly to regain it by using examples from the Book of Mormon and from world and U.S. history. I want to be a mother who prizes freedom and knows it is worth fighting for even when it's my own son or grandson who may be called upon to follow my father's example and defend the United States of America.

If you are not a citizen of the U.S., your country is a promised land to you. Celebrate your country's heritage and teach your children to be proud of and thankful for their country.

TEACHING CHILDREN
ABOUT THE SACRAMENT

We teach our children about the sacrament to deepen their testimonies and increase spiritual development. We teach them to be reverent during the sacrament. We teach them to think of Jesus during the sacrament. We teach them the symbolism—that the bread represents Jesus Christ's body and the water His blood. We teach them that it is a privilege for Aaronic Priesthood young men to do what Jesus Himself did—bless and pass the bread and the water. We teach the historic context of the sacrament—that on the night before He was crucified, Jesus introduced the ordinance of the sacrament to His Apostles. "And as they were eating, Jesus took bread, and blessed it, and brake it, and gave it to the disciples, and said, Take, eat; this is my body. And he took the cup, and gave thanks, and gave it to them, saying, Drink ye all of it; For this is my blood of the new testament, which is shed for many for the remission of sins" (Matthew 26:26–28).

We teach about Jesus' visit to what would become America and that He instituted the sacrament to His "other sheep." "And it came to pass that Jesus commanded his disciples that they should bring forth some bread and wine unto him. And while they were gone for bread and wine, he commanded the multitude that they should sit themselves down upon the earth. And when the disciples had come with bread and wine, he took of the bread and brake and blessed it; and he gave unto the disciples and commanded that they should eat. And when they had eaten and were filled, he commanded that they should give unto the multitude" (3 Nephi 18:1–4).

We teach that the Lord told Joseph Smith: "It is expedient that the church meet together often to partake of bread and [water] in the remembrance of the Lord Jesus" (D&C 20:75). On each of these occasions "the elder or priest shall administer it; and after this manner shall he administer it—he shall kneel with the church and call upon the Father in solemn prayer" (D&C 20:76).

After I had taught these facts multiple times to multiple children, I think I mentally crossed "Teach about the sacrament" off my list. But I'm sure you are one step ahead of me and can see that I initially forgot to teach my children the most important aspect of the Lord's supper—that the sacrament is a covenant. I'd been focused on the mechanics and historical aspects only, and maybe that's okay for very young children. Older children, however, need to understand that a covenant is a solemn, two-way promise with our Eternal Father that will never be broken unless we break our part of the covenant. Heavenly Father never breaks His part; it's contrary to His nature.

You know these covenants because they are stated in the sacrament prayers.

I promise to	Heavenly Father promises to
Remember the body and blood of Jesus	Send His Spirit, the Holy Ghost, to be with me always
Be willing to take upon me the name of Jesus	
Always remember Him	
Keep His commandments	

Though our list of promises looks longer, it's a pittance compared to the promise Heavenly Father makes that a member of the Godhead, the Holy Ghost, will always be with us. The companionship of the Holy Ghost assists us in every aspect of our lives and helps us keep our covenants.

At some point, it dawned on me that I also hadn't taught my children the relationship between the Atonement, repentance, and the sacrament. So we added to family home evening lessons and impromptu teaching moments how partaking of the sacrament with prayerful hearts, having repented of the sins we committed during the week, gives us the chance to renew our baptismal covenants and become clean. As our children were preparing for baptism, we taught them what it meant to be accountable and how repentance and the sacrament go hand-in-hand. As they grew up, I found it important to remind them that repentance gives us a claim on the Lord's mercy and that as they "approach the sacrament with the reverence and solemnity it deserves, it becomes a weekly opportunity for introspection, repentance, and rededication—a source of strength and a constant reminder of the Savior's Atonement" (*True to the Faith: A Gospel Reference* [2004], 148).

The action of partaking of the sacrament is so personal and introspective that our children may not know what to do or think of during the sacrament.

We can teach them that as the sacrament prayers begin, we can reverently remember that we have an Eternal Father to whom we can pray. We remember His Son, Jesus Christ, who paid the penalty for our sins, a penalty we won't have to pay if we repent. We remember that we can be washed clean every week by repenting of our sins and partaking of the sacrament. We remember that the bread and water bless and sanctify our souls as we remember the body and blood of Jesus Christ that was sacrificed for us. We remember that as we keep His commandments we are worthy to claim the blessings of this great covenant, the sacrament of the Lord's supper, which is "that they may always have his Spirit to be with them" (D&C 20:77).

TEACHING CHILDREN
ABOUT THE MILLENNIUM

Isaiah 54:13–14 prophesies that the time will come when "righteousness [will] be established," when there will be no "oppression," no "fear," and "terror . . . shall not come near thee," when "all thy children shall be taught of the LORD; and [when] great shall be the peace of thy children." Parents long for the fulfillment of this promise because nothing horrifies them more than sin and its consequences in the lives of those for whom they would give their own lives. Is there a way to hurry the Millennium so that our children and grandchildren can grow up in peace and righteousness? Perhaps a few questions and answers about the Millennium will provide insight and hope.

Q: What is the Millennium?
A: The Millennium is the 1,000-year period that begins with the Second Coming of Jesus Christ (see Revelation 20:4).

Q: Where will Jesus Christ be during the Millennium?
A: "Christ will reign personally upon the earth" (Article of Faith 1:10). "The millennial day is one in which the Lord himself will dwell with men. This is a boon of inestimable worth. We can scarcely conceive of the glory and wonder of it all. The Lord Jesus Christ, the King of heaven, our Savior and Redeemer, the Lord God Omnipotent dwelling among men!" (Bruce R. McConkie, *The Millennial Messiah* [Salt Lake City, UT: Deseret Book Company, 1982], 652).

Q: What will the earth be like during the Millennium?
A: The earth will return to the state it was in before Adam and Eve partook of the fruit of the tree of good and evil. "The earth will be renewed and receive its paradisiacal glory" (Articles of Faith 1:10). Isaiah expounds, "The wolf also shall dwell with the lamb, and the leopard shall lie down with the kid; and the calf and the young lion and the fatling together;

and a little child shall lead them. And the cow and the bear shall feed; their young ones shall lie down together: and the lion shall eat straw like the ox" (Isaiah 11:6–7).

Q: What will life be like during the Millennium?

A: There will be righteous mortals and resurrected Saints from all ages assisting the Lord when He reigns as King of Kings and Lord of Lords. "The work of saving the dead has practically been reserved for the dispensation of the fulness of times, when the Lord shall restore all things. It is, therefore, the duty of the Latter-day Saints to see that it is accomplished. We cannot do it all at once, but will have the 1,000 years of the millennium to do it in. In that time the work must be done in behalf of the dead of the previous 6,000 years, for all who need it. Temples will be built for this purpose, and the labor in them will occupy most of the time of the saints" (Joseph Fielding Smith, *Doctrines of Salvation*, ed. Bruce R. McConkie [Salt Lake City, UT: Bookcraft, Inc., 1955], 2:166).

Q: Will cycles of war and peace continue?

A: No. "They shall beat their swords into plowshares, and their spears into pruninghooks: nation shall not lift up sword against nation, neither shall they learn war any more" (Isaiah 2:4).

Q: Will Satan still have power to tempt and disrupt?

A: No. "And I saw an angel come down from heaven. . . . And he laid hold on . . . Satan, and bound him a thousand years, And cast him into the bottomless pit, and shut him up, and set a seal upon him, that he should deceive the nations no more, till the thousand years should be fulfilled" (Revelation 20:1–3).

Q: What will be the name of Zion's city?

A: "And it shall be called the New Jerusalem, a land of peace, a city of refuge, a place of safety for the saints of the Most High God . . . and it shall be called Zion" (D&C 45:66–67).

Q: Why is the Second Coming referred to as "the great and dreadful day?" How can it be both?

A: It will be a great day for the righteous who are prepared and have anticipated the Second Coming. It will be a dreadful day for the wicked. "For the day soon cometh that all the proud and they who do wickedly shall be as stubble; and the day cometh that they must be burned. For . . . the fulness of the wrath of God shall be poured out upon all the children of men; for he will not suffer that the wicked shall destroy the righteous. . . . Wherefore, the righteous need not fear; for . . . they shall be saved, even if it so be as by fire" (1 Nephi 22:15–17).

Q: Is there a way our personal righteousness can hasten the Second Coming?
A: No, for the time is fixed. Also, it is a depraved and sinful world that will greet the Savior at His coming. The righteous, those with oil in their lamps, will be caught up to meet Him as the wicked are destroyed.

But there is something we can do today to hasten our personal millennium. President Spencer W. Kimball said, "When Satan is bound in a single home—when Satan is bound in a single life—the Millennium has already begun in that home, in that life" (*Teachings of Spencer W. Kimball,* ed. Edward L. Kimball [Salt Lake City, UT: Bookcraft, Inc., 1982], 172). May you each begin your personal millennium, bringing added peace and righteousness to your life and home, by being "faithful, praying always, having your lamps trimmed and burning, and oil with you, that you may be ready at the coming of the Bridegroom" (D&C 33:17).

"MY CUP RUNNETH OVER WITH LOVE"

There is an old musical called *I Do! I Do!* that includes a song titled "My Cup Runneth Over." This song is a sweet expression of a man's profound love for his wife. If you don't have a husband, let alone one who can express his gratitude to you in such tender words, you can still have the experience of having your heart running over with love. While you are waiting for your Prince Charming to ride in on his white horse and sweep you off your feet (yeah, right!) and the years are accumulating, there may be days you are a little angry about not having "Mrs." before your name. One of my dear friends is resigned to the fact that her husband isn't going to show up in mortality. She jokes that he was too pure to stay on earth and died in infancy. Even though she may joke about it, it is her absolute faith that she will yet meet the man she is to marry either here or on the other side of the veil.

The joys and challenges of marriage might not come to her in this life, but another aspect of marriage can be hers. She still can have opportunity to have children in this life to warm her heart and bring a smile to her face. You would say she is single, having no husband and no children, but she has about twenty-five children each year. Her mothering skills and inclinations to nurture find fulfillment five days a week in her fourth-grade classroom. Another friend is the first person to greet you when you enter "her" museum on a large university campus. With no husband and no children, she temporarily adopts those who come with a need she can fill. Her genuine love literally flows from her. The joy of teaching children is the brightest aspect of her life. Another friend has taught music lessons to hundreds, some of whom now include her in every aspect of their lives. No husband doesn't mean no children.

There are so many wonderful women who mother others' children in Primary classrooms around the world. This kind of mothering has many of the perks and few of the risks of actual motherhood. If you make mistakes, you don't have to live with the consequences. You get to experiment on other people's children. I want to thank the women who have mothered my children.

I hope you know who you are and feel good about bringing joy into their lives. To have precious experiences with children, you just have to be around them. Whether you are a mother because you actually gave birth to a child or because you have been blessed to adopt a child or because you are an aunt to a child or because you've been blessed to teach a child in school or music or dance or art, you have your own collection of priceless stories. Here are a few of my favorites.

When my sister Rochelle was a young mother with three little children (Amy, age five; Mark Todd, three; and Heidi, a few weeks old), Amy and Mark Todd were helping her prepare a salad for dinner. She got out what they liked in salads: lettuce, carrots, and tomatoes. When Heidi started crying in another room, Rochelle told Amy and Mark Todd that she had to go take care of Heidi but that she would be back in a few minutes. She told them that they could keep working on the salad but not to use the knife. When she returned several minutes later, she saw the lettuce torn up nicely in the bowl with some strange-looking carrots sprinkled on top. Her first reaction was, "They used the knife!" She quickly looked at both children and saw that neither was bleeding and asked, "How did you cut up the carrots?" Amy quickly replied that she had torn up the lettuce and that Mark Todd had done the carrots. "How did you cut up the carrots?" Rochelle asked Mark Todd again. "I told you not to use the knife!"

"I didn't use the knife, Mommy," he assured her.

"Then how did you cut the carrots?"

"I used my teeth," he said proudly. "I bit the carrot and then put the pieces in the salad."

Her cup runneth over with love.

My brother Russ tells of the time he had finally, finally finished his residency in Arizona, gotten a job in Utah, and bought their first home. When he and his wife returned from purchasing the house, he took six-year-old Megan on his lap and said, "You're going to love our new house. If you look out the windows on the east, you'll see beautiful mountains. If you look out the windows on the west, you'll see a beautiful lake. You can choose. On which side would you like your bedroom?" With only a second of thought Megan said, "Which side will I be able to watch for you to come home from work on?" His cup runneth over with love.

I was watching my five-year-old grandson, Ben. After his mother drove away, he said, "Grandma, do you have anything that needs to be done? Because I am here." My cup runneth over with love.

One Sunday, my six-year-old grandson, John, came with the rest of his family for Sunday dinner. As I hugged each of the children, John looked at me with very serious eyes and said he had something he *had* to talk to me about. Whatever it was seemed so pressing that I took him into another room to find out what was on his mind. "Grandma," John said, "will you come to my church sometime?" I explained to him that Sundays were especially busy days for Grandpa and me, but sure, we could go with him sometime. "That's great," John said. "We belong to the true Church and I want you and Grandpa to belong to the true Church too. We have a prophet and the Book of Mormon and CTR rings." Suddenly I realized that John thought that because we went to different wards that we belonged to different churches. Evidently the missionaries had come to Primary and told the children that they were not too young to be missionaries. They had challenged the children to think of someone who would make a good member of Jesus' Church and challenged them to talk to that person this week, and John thought of me! My cup runneth over with love.

I went to my grandchildren's annual Primary sacrament meeting presentation. The Primary president began the program by telling of her love for each child. She read in 3 Nephi about Jesus blessing the children: "And he took their little children, one by one, and blessed them, and prayed unto the Father for them. And when he had done this he wept again; And he spake unto the multitude, and said unto them: Behold your little ones" (3 Nephi 17:21–23). The Primary president looked up from reading and said, "Primary children, will you now come and take your places?" As the children reverently began to move out of their seats in the congregation and to fill the choir seats, she said to the congregation, "Behold your little ones." My cup runneth over with love.

Jesus Christ said, "Except ye be converted, and become as little children, ye shall not enter into the kingdom of heaven" (Matthew 18:3). No matter how old or young you are, no matter whatever else is going on in your life, learn to be childlike by finding ways to spend time with children, and, on occasion, there will be moments when your cup will run over with love.

DOES THE LORD KNOW YOUR NAME?

On a beautiful spring morning in the year 1820, the heavens opened, and God the Father and His Son Jesus Christ appeared to Joseph Smith. "When the light rested upon me I saw two Personages, whose brightness and glory defy all description, standing above me in the air. One of them spake unto me, *calling me by name . . .*" (Joseph Smith—History 1:17; emphasis added). Joseph's purpose that morning was to find out which church was right. That question was answered and many other truths were simultaneously taught. For a fourteen-year-old boy, it must have been comforting just to know that his Father in Heaven knew him by name. Have you ever wondered, *Does Heavenly Father know me by name, too?*

Names are significant to the Lord. In the Pearl of Great Price we learn the Lord named Adam. "And the first man of all men have I called Adam" (Moses 1:34). Then Adam was asked to give a name to the woman God had given him. "And Adam called his wife's name Eve; because she was the mother of all living" (Genesis 3:20). We even learn that it was important for the animals to have names. "And Adam gave names to all cattle, and to the fowl of the air, and to every beast of the field" (Genesis 2:20).

Joseph, who was sold into Egypt, knew by revelation thousands of years before Joseph Smith was born that the Prophet of the Restoration would be named Joseph like himself and that his father's name would also be Joseph (see 2 Nephi 3:15). Josiah's name is prophesied of in the Old Testament more than 250 years before he was born (see 1 Kings 13:2). The Lord knew Jeremiah before he was born (see Jeremiah 1:5).

When the babe was born to Elisabeth and Zacharias, relatives expected the baby boy to be named after his father, but Zacharias, who had been struck dumb for doubting the angel's words, had been told the baby's name. Zacharias wrote, "His name is John" (Luke 1:63). The angel Gabriel told Mary to name her firstborn son Jesus. We know many of His other names. Isaiah wrote, "and his *name* shall be called Wonderful, Counsellor, The mighty God,

The everlasting Father, The Prince of Peace" (Isaiah 9:6; emphasis added). We know He was known as Jehovah in the Old Testament (see Exodus 6:3).

The scriptures document the loving, personal way in which the Lord uses names. He called, "Abraham, Abraham" (Abraham 1:16), "Moses, Moses" (Exodus 3:4), "Samuel, Samuel" (1 Samuel 3:10), and "Martha, Martha" (Luke 10:41). He called Zacchaeus by name and said, "make haste, and come down [from the tree]; for to day I must abide at thy house" (Luke 19:5). He knew Isaiah's name and even paid him a compliment when he said, "Great are the words of Isaiah" (3 Nephi 23:1). He used Helaman's son Nephi's name in a most beautiful way: "Behold, thou art Nephi, and I am God" (Helaman 10:6). Jesus called His Apostles in Jerusalem and His disciples in the New World by name. He called Enos by name when He forgave his sins (see Enos 1:5). Near the garden tomb, Jesus gently said the name of Mary (see John 20:16).

Family history work is all about names. Temple work is all about names. The first words said when a person receives a blessing or is set apart to a calling are his or her given names. What are the first words said when a person is baptized and confirmed? His or her name. In the book of Revelation, we learn that the righteous will be given "a white stone, and in the stone a new *name* written, which no man knoweth saving he that receiveth it" (Revelation 2:17; emphasis added).

The fact that you and I know the names of all of our children and grandchildren seems an obvious fact, but as children of a God who allows us the privilege of minute-by-minute communication with Him, how could He not know our names as well as we know the names of our children? He knows our families and our concerns so that when we pray for Donna or Bob or Mom or Michael, He knows to whom we are referring. For this reason a prayer roll makes perfect sense—He knows His children by name.

By the same reasoning, it seems impossible that Jesus Christ could be our personal advocate with the Father and not know each of us by name. "If any man sin, we have an advocate with the Father, Jesus Christ the righteous" (1 John 2:1). Can you imagine the thrill it will be to hear Heavenly Father or Jesus Christ call you by name?

We begin every petition to Heavenly Father with His name. We honor the name of God our Eternal Father and speak His name with deep reverence; anything less is profane. This is one way we can separate ourselves from the rest of the world who blasphemously use His name in nearly every sentence. Jesus Christ Himself taught us the reverential and deferential way we should say His Father's name. After addressing Him as "Our Father which art in heaven," Jesus said, "Hallowed [which means holy, sanctified, blessed, sacred] be thy *name*" (Luke 11:2; emphasis added).

With this same reverence we honor the hallowed name of Jesus Christ, using it only with the deepest devotion and respect. We take upon ourselves

His name at baptism and weekly as we partake of the sacrament. We use His sacred name, acknowledging His role as our mediator with the Father as we close every prayer and end every testimony. We are careful to end our prayers and testimonies not as a way to say, "I'm finished," but to do justice to the name of our Savior in a deliberate and unhurried expression of awe, "in the name of Jesus Christ."

Do Heavenly Father and Jesus Christ know our names? Yes, and we, with gratitude and veneration, are blessed to know Theirs.

WILL THE LORD
STRENGTHEN YOU?

After vigorously preaching repentance to the unresponsive Nephites, Nephi was returning home, "being much cast down because of the wickedness of the people of the Nephites, their secret works of darkness, and their murderings, and their plunderings, and all manner of iniquities" (Helaman 10:3). "He was thus pondering in his heart," probably trying to reconcile what he felt the Lord expected of him compared to what he wasn't accomplishing.

Haven't you been there, trying to do the Lord's work, vigorously serving in your calling, meeting opposition, and feeling depleted of strength? Perhaps you are struggling with how to get your Sunday School class of seven thirteen-year-olds to be attentive. Perhaps you are trying to help your counselors work more harmoniously with each other. Perhaps you feel frustrated because your visiting teaching companion doesn't return your phone calls. Perhaps you struggle with a husband who is inactive or parents who aren't members of the Church, or friends who belittle your testimony or criticize the time you spend on your calling or your desire to have a family. Perhaps you struggle with chronic health problems that somehow make you feel guilty that you can't serve more. Perhaps you are married to a good man, but he is lost in his work, or critical of you, or impatient with your children, or unsupportive of you in your calling. Perhaps there's nothing specific; you just feel inadequate in general. You can identify with Nephi's "being cast down," and going towards home with a dejected, rejected, heavy heart, because you've been there. I've been there. You've tried to do what the Lord assigned; you've tried to serve at home and in your callings, but like Nephi, you have felt or feel that your service isn't enough. You've persevered, endured, and continued, but you're tired and hungry and want to put your feet up and stop the world for a while.

A woman was suffering with the imminent deaths of two family members—one very old and one very young. She was a weary counselor in Young Women, a tired mother of five, a fatigued bookkeeper for her husband's business. Then she got word that the bishop had called a special meeting for the presidencies of the Relief Society, Young Women, and Primary. She wanted to stay home but felt the Spirit coaxing her to attend. Perhaps the bishop was going to say thank you for all her hard work. She needed that. She arrived at the meeting expecting to be rewarded with gentle, inspiring words to lift her spirits. Soon, remarkably ungentle words were hitting her. "You are capable of more," the bishop was saying. "It's easy to feel put upon. It's convenient to feel you are working to your maximum potential, but you are really allowing yourself to do less than you can."

Stop! she felt like screaming. *Don't you realize I'm doing my best?* But he continued on, pressing the idea of doing and becoming more. He talked about spiritual potential, less fluff in things that don't really matter, attention to and following promptings, and five minutes more on your knees or in the scriptures.

As the woman told her story, she said at first she was angry at the bishop and felt under-appreciated. Yet, a little voice within begged her to consider that maybe, just perhaps, he was right. She asked herself whether she thought it was her right to feel weary because of all that was going on in her life. She thought of a conversation she had recently had with some friends—a conversation that had turned into a one-upmanship complaining session. Could it be fashionable to complain and feel weary? Was feeling weary an excuse to complain? Then she said she began to think that in nearly all aspects of her life, there was much, much more to be happy about than there was to be distressed over. She began to think of ways to make better use of her time, her thoughts, her energy, her talents, her leisure.

The bishop read from Helaman 10, telling about how Nephi, son of Helaman, was "cast down" as he made his way toward home after an exhausting and unproductive day (Helaman 10:3). He told what happened to give Nephi the strength to continue. The bishop ended the evening by saying the closing prayer himself, praying that each woman who was present would have an added measure of the Lord's strength. On her way home, even though she felt she had cause to feel down, she decided to pray for the Lord to strengthen her as He had Nephi.

In the *Ensign* article "Heeding the Voice of the Prophets" (July 2008, 4), President Dieter F. Uchtdorf asked a question of us referencing the scriptural idea of running beyond one's strength. He was making another point, but I felt that the Spirit was asking me directly, "Are you running beyond your strength?" The words "your strength" jumped out for me. Of course I will run out of strength if I am just using my own. Man's strength depletes; the Lord's strength replenishes. It's an established pattern in scripture: you give the Lord your strength, and He gives you His strength.

Moses knew: "And Moses said unto the people . . . for by strength of hand the LORD brought you out from this place . . ." (Exodus 13:3). The Lord's strength brings you out of bondage.

King David knew: "The LORD will give strength unto his people; the LORD will bless his people with peace"(Psalm 29:11). The Lord's strength gives you peace.

Isaiah knew: "But they that wait upon the LORD shall renew their strength; they shall mount up with wings as eagles; they shall run, and not be weary; and they shall walk, and not faint" (Isaiah 40:31). The Lord renews strength.

Daniel knew: "I have retained no strength. . . . For . . . straightway there remained no strength in me, neither is there breath left in me. Then there came again and touched me one like the appearance of a man, and he strengthened me, And said, O man greatly beloved, fear not: peace be unto thee, be strong, yea, be strong. And when he had spoken unto me, I was strengthened" (Daniel 10:16–19). The Lord loves you. He will give you faith; He will give you peace; He will make you strong.

Nephi, son of Lehi, knew: "But it came to pass that I prayed unto the Lord, saying: O Lord, according to my faith which is in thee, wilt thou deliver me from the hands of my brethren; yea, even give me strength that I may burst these bands with which I am bound. And it came to pass that when I had said these words, behold, the bands were loosed from off my hands and feet" (1 Nephi 7:17–18). The Lord will give you strength to break the bonds that bind you.

Alma knew: "O Lord, wilt thou give me strength, that I may bear with mine infirmities. For I am infirm, and such wickedness among this people doth pain my soul. . . . O Lord, wilt thou grant unto me that I may have strength, that I may suffer with patience these afflictions which shall come upon me, because of the iniquity of this people. . . . And the Lord provided for them that they should hunger not, neither should they thirst; yea, and he also gave them strength, that they should suffer no manner of afflictions, save it were swallowed up in the joy of Christ. Now this was according to the prayer of Alma; and this because he prayed in faith" (Alma 31:30–31, 38). As you pray in faith, you will be strengthened to bear your infirmities, your afflictions, and the wickedness that surrounds you.

Mormon knew: "And it came to pass that when they had fled we did pursue them with our armies, and did meet them again, and did beat them; nevertheless the strength of the Lord was not with us; yea, we were left to ourselves, that the Spirit of the Lord did not abide in us; therefore we had become weak like unto our brethren" (Mormon 2:26). If you don't have the Lord's Spirit, your strength fails you and leaves you like others who are without the Spirit of the Lord.

Joseph Smith knew: "O GOD, where art thou? And where is the pavilion that covereth thy hiding place? How long shall thy hand be stayed, and thine eye, yea thy pure eye, behold from the eternal heavens the wrongs of thy people and of thy servants, and thine ear be penetrated with their cries? Yea, O Lord, how long shall they suffer these wrongs and unlawful oppressions, before thine heart shall be softened toward them, and thy bowels be moved with compassion toward them?" (D&C 121:1–3). The Lord's answer: "And if thou shouldst be cast into the pit, or into the hands of murderers, and the sentence of death passed upon thee; if thou be cast into the deep; if the billowing surge conspire against thee; if fierce winds become thine enemy; if the heavens gather blackness, and all the elements combine to hedge up the way; and above all, if the very jaws of hell shall gape open the mouth wide after thee, know thou, my son, that all these things shall give thee experience, and shall be for thy good. The Son of Man hath descended below them all. Art thou greater than he?" (D&C 122:7–8). With the Lord's help we are strengthened to be equal to any challenge. Our adversities give us experience and strength and "shall be for [our] good."

I know: There have been many times when I've used up all my strength. Like Nephi, son of Helaman, I've been mentally and physically fatigued, and then the Lord, through a tender mercy, has thanked me for and accepted my efforts. It happened in a remarkable way to Nephi, son of Helaman. "It came to pass as he was thus pondering in his heart, behold, a voice came unto him saying: Blessed art thou, Nephi, for those things which thou hast done; for I have beheld how thou hast with unwearyingness declared the word, which I have given unto thee, unto this people. And thou hast not feared them, and hast not sought thine own life, but hast sought my will, and to keep my commandments" (Helaman 10:3–4).

The Lord didn't chastise Nephi for "being much cast down," but accepted his best efforts because he served with unwearyingness. What a compliment from the Lord! "You've served with unwearyingness" sounds like a synonym for "Well done, thou good and faithful servant" (Matthew 25:21). The Apostle Paul said it this way to the Galatians: "And let us not be weary in well doing: for in due season we shall reap, if we faint not" (Galatians 6:9). The Lord honored Nephi's efforts with added blessings because of his unwearyingness. Said the Lord: "And now, because thou hast done this with such unwearyingness, behold, I will bless thee forever; and I will make thee mighty in word and in deed, in faith and in works. . . . Behold, thou art Nephi, and I am God. . . . And behold, now it came to pass that when the Lord had spoken these words unto Nephi, he did stop and did not go unto his own house, but did return unto the multitudes . . . and began to declare unto them the word of the Lord" (Helaman 10:5–6, 12). Will the Lord strengthen you? You know it!

GIVING GIVES BACK

Have you wondered about the Savior's statement, "Give, and it shall be given unto you; good measure, pressed down, and shaken together, and running over, shall men give into your bosom. For with the same measure that ye mete withal it shall be measured to you again" (Luke 6:38)? I have thought about it and I don't understand how it works—I just know it's true. When I give, I get back. When I hold back, something is withheld from me.

I have a haunting illustration: When I was a young mother, as if that is an excuse for not responding to someone's need, a friend called me and told me her husband had left her. She asked me, since we had children in the same grades, if they could play together sometimes after school. She told me it would help her because she was starting a part-time job three afternoons a week, working out of her home. I talked to my children, and they made an effort to walk home from school with them and invited them over a few times. A few months later she called and asked if I'd teach her how to make bread. I told her to come over and we'd make some. We did, and a few more months passed by. I noticed that her attendance at church was not as regular and I tried to call her a few times. And after a few more months, I was assigned as her visiting teacher. She seemed distant during our visits, and after a couple of months, my visiting teaching assignment changed. *I've got to remember to be her unofficial visiting teacher,* I thought. And then a few years passed by. Today this sister is happily remarried and has wonderfully successful children. But because I only halfheartedly gave a few times instead of wholeheartedly giving when she needed me, our paths slowly stopped crossing until I lost confidence in my ability to be her friend. It's a regret I carry. I feel sorrowful and selfish that I didn't do more. It's almost as if she said to me, "I needed you and you didn't help me. I don't need you anymore."

In contrast, after I had my last chemotherapy treatment, Richard had a conference in St. George, Utah, and asked me to go with him. I knew the change would be good for me, but I felt dull, my skin looked green, I weighed ninety-five pounds, and I doubted that I'd be a very good companion, but he said he wanted me along anyway. So I went. From the hotel window I could see the St. George Temple several blocks away. *That's what I need,* I thought. *I'll walk over and sit on the grounds or in the visitors' center until I can feel the Spirit.* I didn't know if other cancer patients had this problem, but I felt weary and dreary, and although I felt I had been spiritually sustained through my cancer treatments, I felt the Spirit had been muted in me. (Only later as I returned to health did I realize that chemo-induced depression is a very common side effect of chemotherapy.) After spending several hours on the temple grounds and in the visitors' center, I felt marginally better yet somewhat disappointed that I didn't feel a great deal better. As I was returning to the hotel I decided to walk through a few stores. I was their only customer. Glancing around the last store, I saw a woman at a desk surrounded by what looked like piles of bills. I moved away out of her line of sight, feeling like I was intruding on a bleak moment. A couple of minutes later I heard her make a phone call, asking whoever answered the phone to bring her a sandwich since she had forgotten to bring a lunch and it was already 2:30 p.m. As the conversation continued, I could tell she was talking to her husband. He obviously said that he couldn't. "Please," she whispered, thinking I was out of earshot, "there're a couple of slices of turkey in the refrigerator." Evidently, he refused again. I heard her sigh and hang up the phone. As I continued toward the hotel, I walked past a sandwich shop, went in, ordered a turkey sandwich that came with chips and a drink, and took it back to the shop and put it on her desk. The look on her face was more thanks than I ever expected. I felt spiritually full and emotionally satisfied. Giving gives back.

Paula, a college student, told of the hectic morning she spent trying to pack, clean the apartment, and study for finals. Her first year at university was nearly behind her, but she had too much to do and too little time. She was standing at the sink washing of a pile of dirty dishes when she heard a knock at the door.

"Hi, Paula. Do you mind if I come in?"

"No, come in. I'm glad for a break from these dishes."

"I'm ready for a break, too, but from finals," her visitor said. "I wish I had time to talk. I just ran over to borrow a plate."

"A plate?"

"Well, you know, with the hassle of everyone packing, we need an extra one."

Paula thought the request was a little odd but reached into the cupboard for a plate. The only one there was a warped pink plastic plate that had seen the inside of the microwave too many times. She assumed her neighbor wasn't planning to use the plate for anything more important than just eating lunch, but even so, warped pink plastic didn't seem right.

Hesitating, she glanced down in the sink and saw the only china plate they had in the apartment waiting to be washed. Her grandma had given it to her the day she left for college. *Why not,* she thought and quickly washed and dried the plate.

"Here you go. Good luck on finals," Paula said, handing her neighbor the plate.

"Thanks. I'll bring it back soon," was the reply.

As Paula went back to the sink, she remembered a story: A happy, industrious people lived on an island in the ocean. In the middle of the island was a tall and wide mountain, so high and so wide that no villager had ever climbed over it or around it. On the other side of this island lived another happy, industrious people who had also never been able to climb over or around the mountain. Each community lived unaware of the other's existence. One day the people on the first side of the island were a bit too industrious and had produced an excess of garbage. They held a council to decide what to do about the matter. They decided to fill some canoes with the garbage and push them out to sea. Unfortunately, the ocean currents around the island were such that once the canoes floated out of sight, they were pulled around to the other side of the island. The next morning as the happy people on the other side were waking up, they smelled a foul odor in the air and noticed several canoes on the horizon. The chief and his advisors went out to investigate. A few days later, the people on the first side of the island were getting ready to begin their work when they noticed several canoes nearing the island. Soon the villagers realized that these were the same canoes they had sent out to sea. "Oh, no," some cried out. "Our garbage has come back!" But then as they watched, the wind changed. Instead of a putrid smell, a sweet scent filled the air. Instead of garbage, the canoes were filled with fruit and flowers and incense. On the leading canoe was a sign: WE, TOO, SEND OUR VERY BEST.

That's a great story, Paula mused, as a knock at the door interrupted her thoughts. It was her neighbor again. She smiled and handed the plate to Paula without saying a word. On the plate were six large, warm cinnamon rolls, framed beautifully by the china plate.

The question remains, did it matter that Paula didn't just hand her friend the pink plastic plate? Yes, it did to her! Even if the plate had been returned empty, as she expected, she was unselfish, kind, and giving. That busy day, she gave herself a gift: the confidence that she had given her best. It's an eternal law—the law of reciprocity that our Savior taught in many situations. "Go with him twain" (Matthew 5:41). Turn the other cheek (see Matthew 5:39). Do unto others (see Matthew 7:12). "Give, and it shall be given unto you" (Luke 6:38).

Withholding friendship, compliments, talents, or means deprives us of friendships, compliments, talents, and means. My lack of giving has given me a lifetime of regret in a friendship lost. Giving sustains us, blesses us, and gives us the confidence that we have given our best. Giving gives back.

HOPE FOR A BETTER WORLD

When I found a lump in my breast, I hoped it would go away. When it didn't, I hoped it wouldn't be malignant. When it was malignant, I hoped it wouldn't be in the lymph nodes. When it was in the lymph nodes, I hoped the cancer hadn't metastasized. When it mercifully hadn't metastasized, I hoped my hair wouldn't fall out during chemotherapy. When my hair did fall out, I hoped it would grow back in. I heard someone say that hope is just postponing disappointment. How terribly negative and what limited vision. I learned through cancer to hope, hope, and hope again. Cancer and other adversities have proven to me that hope is energy—a renewable source of power that will never diminish. There is more hope available to the human race than can ever be used up, an eternal supply that cannot be depleted. The more you use hope, the more you can have.

Hope is a divine commodity. Hope, as a principle of the gospel, is one of the big three—faith, hope, and charity. Hope, as defined by Moroni, is more than hoping it won't rain or even that a lump will disappear—it is the opposite of despair. "And if ye have no hope ye must needs be in despair" (Moroni 10:22). During my adversities, I've learned that a new hope can be born every second. When there is nothing else, there is always hope. Despair depletes; hope rejuvenates.

A woman who had two of her four sons taken suddenly—one just ready to serve a mission and the other a young father—said, "I know that adversity, as strange as it sounds, brought me to an awareness, perhaps a remembrance, that Heavenly Father loves me more than I thought and is more aware of me than I could have ever anticipated. He gave me comfort and taught me how to hope. This hope is so real that I can share it with, in some cases transfer it to, others who are feeling hopeless."

Like this sister, my hope is centered in the plan of salvation, the great plan of happiness. Knowing that you and I and every person who now lives, has lived, and will yet live on the earth are eternal beings with limitless potential is my fountain of hope. With that understanding and knowledge and testimony, I know that hope works for this very minute, two weeks from yesterday, next year, and decades beyond. Pray for hope. Store hope. Deposit hope. Cling to hope.

Hope is a gift of the Spirit. James 1:5–6 explains the process of asking for and receiving spiritual gifts: "If any of you lack wisdom, let him ask of God." That's the pattern. If any of you lack wisdom or any other spiritual gift such as hope, patience, discernment, or charity, "let him ask of God, that giveth to all men liberally, and upbraideth not; and it shall be given him. But let him ask in faith, nothing wavering. . . ."

Another foundation of hope for me is the fact that Jesus Christ came to earth, obscurely, as a baby and that He will come again, a second time, triumphantly, as a God. That is my faith and my hope. Like the first principle of the gospel, faith in the Lord Jesus Christ, hope is also founded on Christ. Both the plan of salvation and the anticipation of the Second Coming provide foundations for hope—and hope, like faith, to become active in our lives, needs to be centered or focused on something or someone. What is it that we should hope for?

We are instructed in scripture to hope for a better world: "Wherefore, whoso believeth in God might with surety hope for a better world" (Ether 12:4). What is our ultimate hope for a better world? The answer, of course, is that the Second Coming of Jesus Christ will bring a better world. But in my day-to-day mundaneness, I can sometimes forget. I forget that my purpose is to labor to build the kingdom of God on the earth in preparation for the Second Coming of Jesus Christ. We can hope it comes quickly so that our children and grandchildren will grow up without sin, when there will be no accident, no illness, no contention, no anger, no pain, no hatred, no crime, no war, no natural calamities. This blessing, however, will happen after some dreadfully unpleasant prophesied events.

Reading scriptural prophecy of the events preceding the Second Coming may cause anxiety and fear, and the Lord's actual coming will be a "dreadful" time for the wicked. But it will also be a "great" day for the righteous. As we move toward the actual "great" moment of His return, however, even the right-eous will suffer with the wicked through the violence of nature and man. We will have to be hopeful as these tumultuous times unfold. The good news is that each passing day brings us one day closer to His coming. And come He will! A hymn we sing at Christmastime is really a song to be sung in anticipa-tion of the Savior's Second Coming: "Joy to the world, the Lord is come; Let earth receive her King!" ("Joy to the World," *Hymns,* no. 201). Remembering and planning for this glorious event can provide us with sufficient hope to muddle through whatever we are mired in today.

Hope today that the lumps in your life will disappear, and if they don't, hope again and again and again. Specifically hope "For the time soon cometh that the fulness of the wrath of God shall be poured out upon all the children of men; for he will not suffer that the wicked shall destroy the righteous. Wherefore, he will preserve the righteous by his power, even if it so be that the fulness of his wrath must come, and the righteous be preserved, even unto the destruction of their enemies by fire. Wherefore, the righteous need not fear" (1 Nephi 22:16–17). John the Apostle ends the book of Revelation with Jesus Christ's own words: "I am Alpha and Omega, the beginning and the end, the first and the last. . . . Surely I come quickly" (Revelation 22:13, 20). Then John writes five final hope-filled words: "Even so, come, Lord Jesus" (Revelation 22:20).

THE GORILLA DETECTOR

Daniel J. Simons, PhD, of Cornell University studies visual perception and attention. I saw a video of one of his experiments in which a presenter asks an auditorium full of participants to watch Dr. Simons's one-minute video of a basketball game. There are two teams of three who pass a basketball among their own team members. One team wears black shirts, the other white. The presenter instructs the participants to count how many times the white team passes the ball. He says that men and women tend to see a different number of passes and are encouraged to pay careful attention. At the end of the video, the presenter asks how many times the ball was passed. Watching the experiment, I counted seventeen, like many in the auditorium. Then the presenter asked how many saw something unusual occur in the video. Some people raised their hands. I had noticed laughter about halfway through the video but couldn't see any reason for it.

Then the presenter plays the video again. This time he tells the group to forget about counting the number of passes and concentrate on the whole, to see the big picture. The second time, *everyone* sees something unusual. A person in a gorilla suit walks right through the two teams, makes a gorilla-type pounding the chest action—front and center, facing the camera—and walks off. The presenter then explains that there is no difference in how the sexes perform on the test, that he just upped the ante with that statement, actually setting up the audience to miss the gorilla. I immediately felt stupid and less than observant and tried to figure out why I had missed the gorilla. It's probably because I'm competitive and want women to do well in male/female competitions, and I take assignments seriously. If someone tells me to count something, I'm going to count it. But I missed a person dressed up in a silly costume! How can you miss a gorilla?

After viewing the video several more times, I began to doubt my ability to see the world accurately. There must be a difference between *my* world and the *real* world because the real world has gorillas walking around that I don't see. I went to Dr. Simons's Web site and saw some of his other experiments, which again showed how easily our eyes can deceive us. In the gorilla example, the deception began the moment the instruction to count the number of passes was given. It didn't even cross my mind that the instructions were part of the experiment. My husband, on the other hand, whose legal training has taught him to question most everything, saw the gorilla on the first showing. I began to think about what the gorilla symbolizes. There could be many applications, but the one that concerns me personally equates the gorilla with not seeing the whole picture. This is significant because I often include in my prayers a petition to "please help me have the wisdom to see things as they really are."

The gorilla could represent evil and its consequences. Drugs, alcohol, pornography, and gambling—all addictions—are gorillas. All bad habits—selfishness, abruptness, being cantankerous, swearing, gossiping, laziness, dodging responsibility, to name only a few, are gorillas. However, there are many good gorillas that bless and enrich our lives. Being alerted to a talent we didn't know about or being given an opportunity we didn't expect are gorillas for which we give thanks. Everything "virtuous, lovely, or of good report or praiseworthy" (Articles of Faith 1:13) is a good gorilla. Understanding the gorilla factor means we admit our inability to see things as they really are and that we need help, both human and divine.

Having a spouse, sister, mother, friend, coworker, or even stranger alert you to things you are missing, good and bad, is like having a gorilla detector. One time I flew into Oakland, California, to help my daughter while her husband was out of town. I had to take BART (Bay Area Rapid Transit) from the airport to Pleasanton, where they lived. I'd never been on BART. My only experience with trains was on the underground in London, where I became quite proficient at getting where I needed to go by transferring from train to train. So I walked down into the BART station, scanned the walls for signs telling me which train to take, and immediately heard the rumble of an approaching train. I wasn't prepared. The warning lights began to flash, and I looked around for someone to ask which train went to Pleasanton, but there was no one within earshot. The train screeched to a stop, the doors automatically opened, and there I stood, paralyzed with indecision, looking up and down the track for some indication of what I should do. The seconds passed. Just as the train was about to pull away from the station, a man who must have been watching me out of a window left his seat, ran to the open door nearest him, and yelled, "There's only one train. Get on the train!" Thankfully I jumped aboard. How did he understand my dilemma? You know the answer: he had experience. Experience is what gives us wisdom, whether it's counting passes or knowing which train to take. Experience applied helps us make good decisions, and when we share knowledge from our experience, we become gorilla detectors, alerting others to dangers or opportunities they would otherwise miss.

My problem when I don't see the gorilla, whether it's a negative or a positive, is that I may not believe you saw a gorilla either. Imagine seeing the one-minute video for the first time with someone you trust, like a spouse or good friend. You don't see the gorilla but the other person does. The video is over and you say, "I counted seventeen passes; how many did you get?" Your spouse or friend says, "You're kidding, right? It doesn't matter how many passes you counted. It's all about the gorilla." You say, "What gorilla?" He says, "What gorilla! You didn't see the gorilla?" And an hour later you are still arguing about whether or not there was a gorilla.

In real life there are no replays. We can't rewind situations where we miss a gorilla so that we can view the event objectively. What's the solution? I know what it is for me. With humility, I must admit that I will not see every gorilla in my life. I must be willing to believe others who are trustworthy when they tell me the gorilla is real. And I must be thankful for their bravery in telling me what I have missed. Wouldn't it be nice if I said, "Was there a gorilla? Tell me what he looked like so I can watch for him the next time. I'm so thankful you saw him."

ANTIDOTES AND ALTERNATIVES TO WORRY

The Apostle Paul prophesied, "In the last days perilous times shall come" (2 Timothy 3:1). Latter-day prophets have stated that these are the last days, and today's radio, television, newspaper, and Internet stories certainly confirm: these are perilous times. Hazardous conditions—spiritual, physical, emotional, and intellectual—lurk round every corner. Apostle Melvin J. Ballard (1873–1939) said, "If our eyes were only opened to see the powers that are about us, that seek to influence us, we could not have the courage to walk alone and unassisted. These powers are about us, using their influence for the accomplishment of certain well-defined ends to win the coveted place for their chief, the fallen son of God . . . , Lucifer, the devil" ("Struggle for the Soul" [address delivered in the Salt Lake Tabernacle, 5 May 1928], *New Era,* March 1984, 32). Today's natural perils and the "well-defined ends" of Satan certainly give us plenty to worry about.

For years I've been working on reducing worry because I have a habit of worrying instead of sleeping. Dale Carnegie said, "It's the worry that gets you, not the lack of sleep" (http://www.wow4u.com/worry/). He's right. I try to remind myself that if I have no control over an outcome or if I'm worrying about something in the past, I should stop worrying. I know full well that if I can't change it, worry won't help, and if I can change it, worry won't help. But I can be knee-deep in worry before I realize it. Mary C. Crowley gave a thought-provoking antidote for sleeping more and worrying less: "Every evening I turn my worries over to God. He's going to be up all night anyway" (http://thinkexist.com/quotes/mary_c._crowley/). Irving Berlin wrote words my generation knows well: "When I'm worried and I can't sleep, I count my blessings instead of sheep. And I fall asleep, counting my blessings" ("Count Your Blessings"). The current generation just takes Ambien.

Even though it is natural to worry, worry saps energy, occupies brain space, uses up time, and lowers overall productivity. During periods of worry we remember less, learn less, and are less creative. Chronic worry can become a medical problem. Worry can function as a drug, putting the body on high alert with symptoms such as increased heart rate, sweating, and elevated blood pressure. Dean Smith said, "If you treat every situation as a life-and-death matter, you'll die a lot of times" (http://thinkexist.com/quotes/dean_smith). Worry can even give a little adrenalin rush, which may make our brains want more worry. Worry allows random thoughts to bombard the mind with what-ifs. Worry is unproductive, solutionless, fear-based, and thrives on itself. Worry is not only unhealthy and negative, but can also be contagious, passing from sister to sister or friend to friend. It can also be hereditary, as worry patterns seem to transfer to the next generation.

There is also a good, healthy kind of worry. Sometimes the Spirit has alerted me to situations that need my attention, and the sensation comes as concern, or you could say worry, for that person. One time I found out my neighbor had breast cancer and wasn't telling anyone. I convinced her to let me tell the Relief Society president. When I called the president she said, "So that's why the Spirit's been nagging me to go visit her." Concern is healthy worry that seeks for solutions to problems. It is orderly, as the Lord told Oliver Cowdery: "You must study it out in your mind" (D&C 9:8). This helpful kind of worry examines ideas and solutions, pondering rather than worrying and searching for a plan to bring resolution.

As you analyze when, why, and how you worry, you will be able to reduce bad worry by replacing it with good worry. Like conquering fear with faith, you turn your worries over to God. Trust Him. Thank Him. Acknowledge His goodness to you. Know that He has prepared a way for you. As you remind yourself of the blessings He has given you, as you address Him in loving and faithful prayer, you will find the power and ability to overcome senseless worry.

In one sentence, James Russell Lowell put 99 percent of our useless worries in perspective when he said, "Let us be of good cheer, remembering that the misfortunes hardest to bear are those which will never happen" (www.quotegarden.com/worry). It's probably just that simple. Almost all of the things you worry about won't happen, and the statement contains the powerful antidote, "Be of good cheer," which is a scriptural phrase. Jesus said to the man stricken with palsy, "Be of good cheer; thy sins be forgiven thee" (Matthew 9:2). When the Apostles saw Jesus walking on the water and were afraid, Jesus said, "Be of good cheer; it is I; be not afraid" (Matthew 14:27). Jesus said to His Apostles, "These things I have spoken unto you, that in me ye might have peace. In the world ye shall have tribulation: but be of good cheer; I have overcome the world" (John 16:33). When Paul feared for his life, the resurrected Christ appeared to him and said, "Be of good cheer, Paul" (Acts 23:11). When the flocks of King Lamoni were scattered, his servants thought they would be killed, but Ammon said to them, "My brethren, be of good cheer" (Alma

17:31). When Nephi and all the believers were going to be put to death, the premortal Christ said to him, "Lift up your head and be of good cheer; for behold, the time is at hand, and on this night shall the sign be given, and on the morrow come I into the world" (3 Nephi 1:13). When Joseph Smith and the early leaders feared, Jesus said, "Verily I say unto you, and what I say unto one I say unto all, be of good cheer, little children; for I am in your midst, and I have not forsaken you" (D&C 61: 36). Again when they feared, the Lord Jesus Christ said, "Be of good cheer, and do not fear, for I the Lord am with you" (D&C 68:6). In Section 78:18, Jesus assures us by saying, "Be of good cheer, for I will lead you along."

Bad things have happened to you in the past. Bad things will happen to you in the future, and all the worry in the world won't change anything. But it will rob you of happiness and sleep. If you worry about the past and the future, there will be less joy in the present. Minimize irrational worry in your life as you count your blessings, turn your worries over to God, be faithful instead of fearful, and be of good cheer—an action showing that you truly trust Heavenly Father. Although these are perilous times, you have been sustained in your trials in the past. Know that you will be sustained in your trials in the future.

RECOGNIZING TENDER MERCIES

Evidence that we receive direction and personalized assistance from the Spirit is noticeable as we fulfill our callings in classrooms, temples, presidency meetings, and as we do missionary work and visiting teaching. It is also apparent as we fulfill our responsibilities in the home. These wonderful evidences, or to quote 1 Nephi 1:20, "tender mercies" of the Spirit's attentiveness reward our efforts and remind us just how close the Spirit can be. It seems to be the reason Nephi is writing a record: "But behold, I, Nephi, will show unto you that the tender mercies of the Lord are over all those whom he hath chosen, because of their faith, to make them mighty even unto the power of deliverance" (1 Nephi 1:20) Do you recognize the tender mercies in your life? Do you record them for future generations? As you follow Nephi's example and document your tender mercies, you are actually making a record of your faith and testimony.

As a Relief Society presidency prayed to know if anyone in the ward needed a visit, a less-active sister's face came to the president's mind. After the "amen," the president said, "Why don't we visit Sister Wells?" So she and the Relief Society secretary drove to Sister Wells's home. Brother Wells answered the door and, without saying anything, motioned them into a bedroom where Sister Wells was lying on the bed, looking very ill. "How did you know to come?" she asked.

A Primary teacher prepared her lesson about Joseph Smith's First Vision for the five-year-old children in her class, anticipating that all the children knew the story well. But she found that it didn't matter whether they were hearing it for the first time or whether it was a retelling, because as she began, she felt the sweet accompaniment of the Spirit and saw the eyes of the children look at her in awe and wonder as the Spirit testified to each.

Unexpectedly, a temple worker sitting at her assigned post began to feel her legs cramp. They had never tightened up like this before, and the pain compelled her to give them a little exercise. She painfully stood and took a brief walk down the hall. As she passed the elevator, she noticed that one of the doors was slightly ajar. She looked more carefully and was surprised to see what looked like the wheel of a wheelchair. Upon closer examination, she realized that someone was in the wheelchair and the elevator door was jammed and wouldn't open. Did her legs get stiff so the person on the elevator could be rescued?

A missionary preparing for the day had a question come to mind: "How would you respond if someone asked you why members of your Church wear special underwear?" She immediately recalled an article she had read on the subject and organized her thoughts. Later that day an investigator asked the question. She thanked her Heavenly Father for preparing her with an appropriate answer.

Mariah, who had only lived in the ward for a few years, was assigned to visit teach Bessie, an inactive sister who had been in the ward for forty years. While introducing herself, Mariah told Bessie she was looking forward to being her visiting teacher. Surprised, Bessie tested the statement. "How could you look forward to visiting someone you know nothing about?" Mariah replied, "I've heard your name; I've seen your name. I've really wanted to meet you." Again, Bessie challenged her: "You just say that to everyone. I haven't been to church for twenty years. No one at church speaks of me anymore. You couldn't have heard or seen my name." Mariah searched her brain. She knew she had seen the woman's name. She prayed to respond truthfully, wanting to establish a good relationship with Bessie. Then the Spirit reminded Mariah and she asked, "Bessie, when is your birthday?" "July 25," she answered. "That's where I've seen your name!" Mariah thankfully sighed. "Our names have always been together on the Relief Society birthday list. My birthday is July 25 too!"

One Sunday, Claudia returned to Primary for the first time after being released from her Primary calling six months previously. She had served in Primary for ten straight years and was excited to return and hear her child give a talk. Although she loved her callings in Primary, if asked she wouldn't say that she had felt the Spirit very often. But this Sunday, as she walked through the door, the presence of the Spirit overwhelmed her to the point that she could not hold back the tears.

A few weeks later, Claudia was driving home when a question entered her mind. Shouldn't tender mercies happen at home with her children and husband more frequently? Wasn't that where she fulfilled her most important work and needed the most help? In almost every family prayer, no matter who prayed, the words "and please bless us with Thy Spirit" were usually said. So why didn't she see greater evidence of His Spirit at home? As she pulled into her driveway, Claudia glanced at the clock and was jolted back to reality. She had been gone a little longer than she had planned and hoped her four children had survived. Her oldest, Jordan, who had just turned twelve, had recently started babysitting her siblings. But Jordan's first babysitting experience a few weeks before had not been positive. When Claudia had arrived home she'd found the house a mess and Jordan crying in her room.

Claudia gingerly opened the door, walked in, and put the groceries on the kitchen counter. All was quiet. She couldn't even hear the television. When she walked down the stairs and entered the family room, she saw Jordan in a large overstuffed chair reading aloud to her siblings. The youngest was tucked at her side and the other two were sitting together on the couch with their feet on an ottoman. As she stood in the doorway, basking in the peaceful scene, she recognized the presence of the Spirit, and the words, "The Spirit is no stranger here" came into her mind.

Claudia realized that the Spirit was very present in her home and that tender mercies were actually common occurrences. She remembered her experience of being overcome with the Spirit in Primary and thought, *I just don't recognize tender mercies at home as much because, like with Primary, I've become accustomed to the presence of the Spirit, making the tender mercies less dramatic, perhaps even routine. Shame on me; I must try to never again take evidences of the Spirit's presence for granted.* And then she took time to privately go into the only room in the house where she could ensure privacy, kneeled down, and thanked her Father in Heaven for His Spirit and tender mercies.

"THE WIND DID CONTINUALLY BLOW"

Naomi experienced many difficulties and sadnesses in her life. A severe famine in Judah forced her husband, Elimelech, to move his family to Moab so that he and Naomi and their two sons wouldn't starve. Then, not long after they moved, Elimelech died, and Naomi was left to raise Mahlon and Chilion by herself. When the boys grew into manhood, both Mahlon and Chilion married young women from Moab. Naomi loved her sons' wives, Orpah and Ruth, like daughters, and then Mahlon and Chilion died.

From the Biblical text it seems as though Naomi had not only decided to return to Bethlehem, but was actually on the road with Orpah and Ruth when she realized the enormity of what she was doing to her daughters-in-law. She was taking them to a foreign land much like the famine had taken her to the foreign land of Moab. We can assume they talked it over before they began their journey, but now Naomi was adamant. She stopped and told Orpah and Ruth to go back home: "Go, return each to [your] mother's house: the Lord deal kindly with you, as ye have dealt with the dead, and with me" (Ruth 1:8). When both Orpah and Ruth reiterated their willingness to go with Naomi to Bethlehem, Naomi said again, "Turn again, my daughters, go your way" (Ruth 1:12). Orpah finally saw wisdom in Naomi's counsel and sadly said good-bye. Ruth, on the other hand, steadfastly insisted on staying with Naomi, affirming with some of the most beautiful words in scripture her love for Naomi and her determination to accompany her to Bethlehem (see Ruth 1:16–17).

Naomi lived through a famine, a move to a foreign country, the death of her husband, the stress of raising two sons alone, the deaths of those two sons, and the sadness of sending one of her daughters-in-law away. She didn't know it, but she was on course.

Of the brother of Jared and his people we read, "And it came to pass that they were many times buried in the depths of the sea, because of the mountain waves which broke upon them, and also the great and terrible tempests which were caused by the fierceness of the wind. And it came to pass that when they were buried in the deep there was no water that could hurt them, their vessels being tight like unto a dish . . . ; therefore when they were encompassed about by many waters they did cry unto the Lord, and he did bring them forth again upon the top of the waters. And it came to pass that the wind did never cease to blow toward the promised land while they were upon the waters; and thus they were driven forth before the wind" (Ether 6:6–8).

No matter the adversity, the wind never ceased to blow toward the promised land! Naomi was on course. The Jaredites were on course—they just didn't realize it.

Bart and Debbie had a year of being bounced around in the ocean. Among other adversities, they tried for six months to sell their lovely home in order to downsize. They tried two realtors and kept drastically reducing the price. Finally, they had to back out of the new, smaller home they were having built. Debbie found out that she had two herniated discs in her neck. A son ran over his trumpet with their van. The same van gave out after fifteen years of faithful service. One daughter had a bicycle accident. A second daughter unexpectedly had to have her wisdom teeth removed. A dog bit a third daughter, and a scorpion bit a fourth daughter. Yet and still they love each other and their children and are trying to be a righteous family.

Naomi would have said, "Even though I suffered through a famine, my husband dying, two sons dying, and Orpah going back to her own people, God gave me Ruth!" Debbie would be the first to agree that her problems pale in comparison to Naomi's, but life isn't about who has it the worst. Adversity isn't fun for anyone. But God has kept blowing Bart and Debbie's family toward the promised land, which Psalms 107:30 describes: "Then are they glad because . . . he bringeth them unto their desired haven."

As long as our testimonies are "tight like unto a dish," as the Jaredite barges were, our adversities are not setbacks, but a means of getting us to our own promised lands. "They that go down to the sea in ships, that do business in great waters; These see the works of the LORD, and his wonders in the deep. For he commandeth, and raiseth the stormy wind, which lifteth up the waves thereof. They mount up to the heaven, they go down again to the depths: their soul is melted because of trouble. They reel to and fro . . . and are at their wits' end. Then they cry unto the LORD in their trouble, and he bringeth them out of their distresses. He maketh the storm a calm, so that the waves thereof are still. Then are they glad because . . . he bringeth them unto their desired haven" (Psalms 107:23–30).

During times of adversity we call upon the Lord for assistance and watch and pray that the wind will never cease blowing in the direction we should go. Do we like the "furious wind," the "mountain waves," and the "great and terrible tempests"? No! But how thankful we will be for the direction the adversity took us when we arrive at our promised land.

When through the deep waters I call thee to go,
The rivers of sorrow shall not thee o'erflow,
For I will be with thee, thy troubles to bless,
And sanctify to thee, And sanctify to thee,
And sanctify to thee thy deepest distress.
(Verse 4, "How Firm a Foundation," *Hymns,* no. 85)

STUCK IN TIME, OR THE CASE FOR CONTINUING REVELATION

The first five books of the Bible—Genesis, Exodus, Leviticus, Numbers, and Deuteronomy—are collectively known as the Pentateuch, or Torah. According to Bible chronologies, these books narrate the first 2,500 years of human history.* The rest of the Old Testament, from Joshua to Malachi, tells of God's dealings with His children until about 445 years before the birth of Jesus Christ. The first four books of the New Testament—Matthew, Mark, Luke, and John—tell of Jesus Christ's birth, ministry, and death. These writings end before AD 70.

As amazing as the Pentateuch is, if that were the only scripture we had, we would be reading about a God who hadn't spoken for about 3,500 years. As wonderful as the rest of the Old Testament is, if that were the only scripture we had, we would be reading about a God who hadn't spoken for about 2,500 years. As magnificent as the New Testament is, if it were the only scripture we had—or if that were as far as our scriptures went—we would be following God's instructions to His children who have been dead for about 2,000 years.

What glorious additional knowledge members of The Church of Jesus Christ of Latter-day Saints have! God spoke to prophets in what would become the Americas from 600 BC to AD 421 (not including the Book of Ether). The Book of Mormon contains 1,000 years of God's dealings with His children and is that necessary second witness of Jesus Christ—"in the mouth of two or three witnesses every word may be established" (Matthew 18:16).

The Doctrine and Covenants includes 138 revelations received from Jesus Christ between 1830 and 1918. Through the Prophet Joseph Smith, 133 revelations were given as our Savior reestablished His Church on the earth. The other five were received by Oliver Cowdery, John Taylor, Brigham Young, and Joseph F. Smith. Two Official Declarations received by Wilford Woodruff in 1890 and by Spencer W. Kimball in 1978 are also included. These revelations are "the will of the Lord, . . . the mind of the Lord, . . . the word of the Lord, . . . the voice of the Lord, and the power of God unto salvation" (D&C 68:4).

The Pearl of Great Price, first published in 1851, is a compilation of diverse scriptures. The books of Moses and Matthew came as revelation to Joseph Smith as he was translating—and amending—the Bible. The book of Abraham was translated by Joseph Smith from Egyptian papyri. Joseph Smith—History is Joseph Smith's first-person narrative of the beginnings of the Church in this dispensation. The Articles of Faith are thirteen concise statements of fundamental Church beliefs that Joseph Smith wrote. Number nine reads, "We believe all that God has revealed, all that He does now reveal, and we believe that He will yet reveal many great and important things pertaining to the Kingdom of God."

We know God is not silent! He continues to play an active role in the lives of His children, and He continues to speak to His servants the prophets. Every six months at general conference and more often as needed, latter-day prophets and Apostles reveal God's will to His people. Yes, we believe in continuous communication between God and His prophets here on earth. We are a most blessed and privileged people. We are not stuck in the past. As the Old Testament prophet Amos said, "Surely the Lord GOD will do nothing, but he revealeth his secret unto his servants the prophets" (Amos 3:7). Our prophet today speaks "the will of the Lord, . . . the mind of the Lord, . . . the word of the Lord, . . . the voice of the Lord, and the power of God unto salvation" (D&C 68:4).

*All dates are approximates for illustration.

ACCELERATING
HARVEST TIME

In Old Testament times, modes of transportation were basic. Most people traveled by foot and, if lucky, carried their goods by donkey or camel. Around 3500 BC*, the wheel was invented. Eventually chariots for the rich and carts drawn by horse, donkey, or ox for the poor were bumping along dirt paths. The earliest travel by sea was in canoes. By the time of King Solomon, one-mast sailing ships were hauling goods from port to port. To sail against the wind, however, large oars were needed.

By New Testament times, the Romans had built a network of roads across their empire. The vehicles that traveled these roads were a bit fancier, but the technology was about the same—chariots and carts. Sea travel had improved. As empires desired larger vessels for trade and war, along with greater access to the open ocean, their boat builders slowly figured out the correct proportions for hull size and strength versus additional masts and sails.

At His ascension, Jesus told His disciples, "Go ye into all the world, and preach the gospel to every creature" (Mark 16:15). But the only means they had of obeying His command at this time in history was by foot—human or animal—or by ship, rowing or sailing.

In the Middle Ages, land travel remained much the same, but again the desire to explore, expand, and conquer led to several inventions that advanced sea travel. The Chinese invented the compass, and the Europeans invented the rudder. The Middle Age "modern" ships increased in size and were easier to steer.

As Europe emerged from the Dark Ages, land travel improved minutely. Saddlebags were invented so that a horse could carry supplies as well as a person, and carts became covered wagons. But roads had not improved beyond the Roman highways.

In the 18th century, stagecoaches regularly carried passengers and goods between towns. The first turnpike road was built, taxing the use of roadways. But land travel was still so slow that waterways were thought to be the hope of the future as canals and rivers became the cheapest and most efficient ways to move people and product.

Enter Joseph Smith onto the stage of history. The night he received the plates from Moroni, he and Emma went to the Hill Cumorah in a horse-drawn carriage. Then, what had been fairly static since the beginning of recorded history suddenly changed. With the restoration of the gospel of Jesus Christ, the stone cut out of the mountain without hands started rolling. As the Second Coming of Jesus Christ nears, transportation and communication technology accelerate to fulfill the prophecy "that the time shall come when the knowledge of a Savior shall spread throughout every nation, kindred, tongue, and people" (Mosiah 3:20).

In 1926, Elder Joseph Fielding Smith said, "I do not believe for one moment that these discoveries have come by chance. . . . They have come and are coming because the time is ripe, because the Lord has willed it, and because he has poured out his Spirit on all flesh" (Conference Report, Oct. 1926, 116–117, quoted in Boyd K. Packer and Russell M. Nelson, "Computerized Scriptures Now Available," *Ensign,* Apr. 1988, 72).

In 1974, President Spencer W. Kimball said, "I believe that the Lord is anxious to put into our hands inventions of which we laymen have hardly had a glimpse. . . . King Benjamin . . . called together all the people in the land of Zarahemla, and the multitude was so great that King Benjamin 'caused a tower to be erected, that thereby his people might hear the words which he should speak unto them' (Mosiah 2:7). Our Father in Heaven has now provided us mighty towers—radio and television towers with possibilities beyond compre- hension—to help fulfill the words of the Lord that 'the sound must go forth from this place unto all the world'" ("When the World Will Be Converted," *Ensign,* Oct. 1974, 3).

President Gordon B. Hinckley said, "I am so deeply thankful that we have the wonders of television, radio, cable, satellite transmission, and the Internet. We have become a great worldwide Church, and it is now possible for the vast majority of our members to participate in these meetings as one great family, speaking many languages, found in many lands" ("Living in the Fulness of Times," *Ensign,* Nov. 2001, 4).

From 3500 BC to AD 1820 (5,320 years), little changed in the mode of land travel, sea travel was difficult and dangerous, and air travel was only for the birds. "Go ye into all the world" must have seemed all but impossible. Today, however, a message that once took many months to reach the recipient can now be transmitted in seconds. Travel that used to take months is now accomplished in less than a day. You can breakfast in New York, lunch in L.A, and enjoy dinner in Honolulu.

Laura Ingalls Wilder wrote of her subsistence-level life on the American frontier in the Little House series. You can feel her anxiety as she awaits her father's return from his solitary multi-day hunting trips in the big woods. You can feel her heartache as she believes she'll never see loved ones again because she's moving 200 miles away. If someone had told her that in 150 years her descendants would carry a small device, push a few buttons, and in seconds talk to anyone who had a similar device anywhere in the world, she would have called it either foolishness or a miracle.

As expected, the enemy of the Lord's work meddles in and abuses and misuses new technology, but his perversions are not the topic here. We are simply rejoicing in the opportunity to watch the work of the Lord expand and thanking our Heavenly Father that this same technology that makes worldwide missionary work possible also makes our lives so much easier.

In the 2007 *Church Almanac* there is a forty-page article on technology and the Church by Dr. James B. Allen titled "A Steady Revolution." He writes, "Whereas in the 1950s missionaries still went to their mission fields by train and ocean-going vessels, sometimes taking weeks to arrive, in the year 2000 they went by jet plane, arriving almost anywhere in the world in a matter of hours after leaving a Missionary Training Center. The air travel of General Authorities [is] scheduled by computer many months ahead of time, correlated with the various stake or regional conferences they [are] scheduled to attend."

Brother Allen explains that computer programs have changed almost every facet of how the Church does genealogical research, the temple endowment presentation, membership records, financial reports, and now even temple recommends. He speaks of film and digital technology that puts Church-produced movies on videotape or DVD for home as well as Church use.

Yes, technology allows us to live more comfortably than ever before in history. In our ease, however, we have to remember these lifestyle conveniences are a byproduct of the true purpose for these inventions. "For, verily, the sound must go forth from this place into all the world, and unto the uttermost parts of the earth—the gospel must be preached unto every creature" (D&C 58:64).

You may be wondering at the premise that Joseph Smith's First Vision in 1820 could possibly pinpoint the beginning of this revolution in technology. Jeffrey D. Sachs, a noted economist selected by *Time* magazine as one of the world's hundred most influential people, cites this exact date—1820—in his *New York Times* bestseller *The End of Poverty* (New York: The Penguin Press, 2005). In fact, the date 1820 is used about ten times on pages 26 through 30.

Dr. Sachs writes, "In the period of modern economic growth, however, both population and per capita income came unstuck, soaring at rates never before seen or even imagined. . . . The global population rose more than sixfold in just two centuries, reaching an astounding 6.1 billion people at the start of the third millennium, with plenty of momentum for rapid population growth still ahead. The world's average per capita income rose even faster, . . .

increasing by around nine times between 1820 and 2000. In today's rich countries, the economic growth was even more astounding. The U.S. per capita income increased almost twenty-five-fold during this period, and Western Europe's increased fifteen-fold. . . . If we combine the increases in world population and world output per person, we find an astounding forty-ninefold increase in total economic activity in the world . . . over the past 180 years [from 1820 to 2000]."

Put simply, 1820 is the year when population and productivity of the world began to dramatically advance. 1820! There is measurable purpose and design to the Lord's plan, noted even by an economist who most likely knows nothing about Joseph Smith or the Lord's amazing ways.

*Dates are approximates for illustration.

AN EYEWITNESS INTO THE HEREAFTER

When Joseph F. Smith, oldest son of Hyrum and Mary Fielding Smith, was born on November 13, 1838, his father and his uncle Joseph Smith were jailed in Richmond, Missouri, and mobs were persecuting and driving Church members from Missouri because of Governor Lilburn W. Boggs's order to exterminate the Mormons. To use Thomas Paine's words, these were "times that try men's souls" (*The Crisis,* 1). Joseph F. Smith would have many more such trying experiences.

When he was five, news came from Carthage, Illinois, on June 27, 1844, that his father and Uncle Joseph, for whom he had been named, had been murdered by a mob. Years later, Joseph F. still recalled going to the Joseph and Emma Smith home where the bodies of the martyrs lay in their coffins. "I remember my mother lifting me up to look upon the faces of my father and the Prophet for the last time" (Preston Nibley, *Presidents of the Church* [Salt Lake City, UT: Deseret Book Company, 1974], 183).

When Joseph F. was thirteen, he experienced another severe trial with the death of his mother. "It was in 1852 that my blessed Mother passed away; leaving me fatherless & motherless, but not altogether friendless at the early age of 13 years" (Joseph F. Smith to Samuel L. Adams, 11 May 1888, quoted in Richard Neitzel Holzapfel and R.Q. Shupe, *Joseph F. Smith: Portrait of a Prophet* [Salt Lake City, UT: Bookcraft, Inc., 2000], 20).

Death claimed his firstborn, Mercy Josephine, who was not yet three. He had been up with her all night and said to her in the morning, "My little pet, you did not sleep all night." She replied, "I'll sleep today, Papa." In recalling her words Joseph F. said, "Oh! how those words shot through my heart. I knew, yet I would not fully believe, that she meant the sleep of death. And she did sleep! Oh . . . my heart is nearly broken for the loss of you" (Amelia Smith McConkie, "Grandpapa Joseph F. Smith," *Ensign,* Sept. 1993, 12).

An infant; two adult daughters, Alice and Zina; and his wife, Sarah, died. Then, adding to his sorrow, his son Hyrum died. His granddaughter Amelia said, "Hyrum's death at age forty-nine, in January 1918, was a crushing blow for Grandpapa. Added to the other separations, Hyrum's death added much cause for Grandpapa to ponder, pray, and search the scriptures for answers about the hereafter and associations with loved ones who had passed away" (ibid.).

Further turning President Smith's mind to ponder death was news of war casualties (World War I), ultimately claiming more than 116,000 American lives. Also, there were the shocking reports that millions were dying from what was called the Spanish flu. (In 1918–1919 at least 21 million died worldwide.)

This is the backdrop the grieving prophet Joseph F. Smith was laboring under when, on October 3, 1918, he sat in his room, pondering "the great and wonderful love made manifest by the Father and the Son in the coming of the Redeemer into the world" (see D&C 138:3). Turning in his scriptures to 1 Peter 3:18–20, he said he was "greatly impressed, more than . . . ever . . . before" with what he read (D&C 138:6). In moments, all the suffering of past sorrows was swallowed up in joy as "the eyes of [his] understanding were opened, and the Spirit of the Lord rested upon" him (verse 11). He saw an innumerable group of the spirits of the dead who had been faithful in the testimony of Jesus while they lived in mortality. They were awaiting the coming "of the Son of God into the spirit world" (16). He had broken the bands of death, which meant that each one of them was anticipating his or her own resurrection. "While this vast multitude waited and conversed . . . , the Son of God appeared" (18). Then our Savior and Redeemer preached to the assembly and "their countenances shone, and the radiance from the presence of the Lord rested upon them, and they sang praises unto his holy name" (24). Joseph F. Smith was an eyewitness to Jesus Christ's reception in the world of spirits after the Atonement and His Resurrection!

President Smith began to recognize the individuals in attendance. He saw Adam and "our glorious Mother Eve" (39). He saw prophets of the Old Testament and "the prophets who dwelt among the Nephites" (49). He saw the Prophet Joseph Smith. He saw his father! Then he was privileged to see how the plan of God works. "I beheld that the faithful elders of this dispensation, when they depart from mortal life, continue their labors in the preaching of the gospel. . . . The dead who repent will be redeemed, through obedience to the ordinances of the house of God, And after they have paid the penalty of their transgressions, and are washed clean, shall receive a reward according to their works . . ." (57–59).

We all have lost loved ones to what we call death, but they are just separated from us for a season. They live; they gather together; they converse; they preach the gospel or are preached to. About six weeks after this vision, President Joseph F. Smith joined those who had preceded him into the world of spirits.

But before he left, he recorded this vision, saying, "I know that this record is true" (60).

This is personal for each of us. Life goes on after death and continues in the spirit realm. Through the Atonement of Christ each of us and all who have ever lived on the earth will be resurrected. Our almost unbearable pains of being parted from loved ones will yet yield jubilation when we meet them at Jesus's feet to enjoy their and His company forever.

"WHAT GOES ON INSIDE YOUR LDS TEMPLES?"

Most of you will have opportunity to answer questions about the temple posed by friends who are members of others faiths. Perhaps you have family who are not members of the Church; even your children may have questions. They may be curious about what goes on inside an LDS temple. They may wonder what the difference is between a temple and a ward building. They may wonder why only members of the Church in good standing can go inside the temple. They may be puzzled as to what a temple recommend is and how one is obtained. Hopefully, the following will help you answer these and other questions.

There are two reasons why only faithful members can go inside the temple, and both are because of what happens in the temple. First, the temple is a place where sacred ordinances are performed, such as baptisms and marriages. Secondly, in the temple, members make covenants with God. That's why admittance is restricted. Making covenants with God and participating in sacred ordinances is serious, binding, and sacred. Putting someone in that situation unprepared wouldn't be right.

A temple recommend is like a reusable ticket, certifying that the person whose name is on the recommend has been *recommended* by his or her bishop as one who is worthy to enter the temple. The recommend is shown each time a member wants to go inside a temple.

A ward or stake building is where worship services are held on Sundays. Temples are closed on Sundays. Although both are places of worship, ward and stake buildings are open to the public; everyone is welcome. Activities and parties as well as worship services are held in ward and stake buildings.

The temple has been termed "the Lord's University." Here members are taught about the purpose of this earth life. One of the greatest insights gained is that from Adam to today, God has had the same plan and desire for each of His children who have lived or will yet live upon the earth. From the time of Adam and Eve, God has given men and women the opportunity to make covenants with Him. Early in the history of the world, these covenants were made at altars. From Facsimile No. 2 in the book of Abraham in the Pearl of Great Price, we see that Abraham built an altar according to God's direction. From the Bible we know that Noah and Moses similarly built altars. Later, God commanded Moses to build a tabernacle, which had elements of a portable temple. Then King David obeyed the command the Lord gave him to gather supplies for a temple, and his son, Solomon, was privileged to build the temple. After it was partly destroyed, Zerubbabel was given the opportunity to rebuild it. Fire damaged the temple. Later, Herod the Great, to gain popularity with the Jews, began to rebuild and enlarge the temple. This is the temple in which Jesus discoursed with the doctors at age twelve and where, during His ministry, He drove out the moneychangers with the words, "My house shall be called the house of prayer; but ye have made it a den of thieves" (Matthew 21:13).

In the Book of Mormon we read that temples were built in the lands we know as the Americas. The temple at Bountiful is where Jesus Christ appeared after His crucifixion.

The work done in the temples is beautiful and edifying. The temple is a place of learning and introspection. It provides time for prayer and meditation. The reason members of the Church go to the temple often is because in such an environment, feeling close to the Lord and learning His ways comes more easily.

One of the very best experiences for those who revere the temple is going with a family member or friend for the first time as he or she receives his or her spiritual endowment (a gift or blessing). Another singular experience is to see a man and woman married (sealed or bound together) for time and eternity. This is done by the same authority Jesus gave to His Apostles: "And I will give unto thee the keys of the kingdom of heaven: and whatsoever thou shalt bind on earth shall be bound in heaven" (Matthew 16:19).

Because members of the Church don't talk about what happens in the temple, those who do not belong to the Church may surmise that it's secret, perhaps even cultish. Nothing could be further from the truth. The experience in the temple is sacred, pure, holy, and enlightening in every aspect. We believe temples are literally houses of the Lord. "[The] external appearance [of the temples hints] of its deeply spiritual purposes. . . . Over the door to the temple appears the tribute 'Holiness to the Lord.' When you enter any dedicated temple, you are in the house of the Lord" (Boyd K. Packer, "The Holy Temple," *Liahona,* June 1992, 14).

Even for members of the Church, preparing to go to the temple for the first time or preparing to return after not going for a while can be a challenging process. Again from President Packer: "Curiosity is not a preparation. Deep interest itself is not a preparation. Preparation for the ordinances includes preliminary steps: faith, repentance, baptism, confirmation, worthiness, a maturity and dignity worthy of one who comes invited as a guest into the house of the Lord" (ibid.). In consultation with your bishop, you can learn what steps are needed to prepare and qualify yourself to be within the walls of the House of the Lord.

When Joseph Smith dedicated the temple at Kirtland, Ohio, in 1836, he prayed with words that give us an idea of the power of temples: "Organize yourselves; prepare every needful thing, and establish a house, even a house of prayer, a house of fasting, a house of faith, a house of learning, a house of glory, a house of order, a house of God . . . that thy glory may rest down upon thy people, and upon this thy house, which we now dedicate to thee, that it may be sanctified and consecrated to be holy, and that thy holy presence may be continually in this house; and that all people who shall enter upon the threshold of the Lord's house may feel thy power, and feel constrained to acknowledge that thou hast sanctified it, and that it is thy house, a place of thy holiness" (D&C 109:8, 12–13).

THE GREAT LEVELER
AND ELEVATOR

When you see someone driving down the street, you know what kind of car he or she drives. When you are introduced to someone new, you notice his or her clothes, hairstyle, and jewelry. When a person speaks, you can often assess where he or she is from and, often, what his or her level of education is. These tangible cues allow us to make assumptions about people we meet and can be a distracting influence in getting to know and understand the real person. Happily, there is a place where almost all criteria by which we judge others are eliminated.

In the temple, an individual's level of education doesn't matter. There is no opportunity to use complex vocabulary, explain theories, or expound knowledge. No one comes to the temple to teach, only to be taught. A nuclear scientist could sit between an individual with an eighth-grade education and a famous composer, and no one would know the difference. A person who has been a member of the Church for just one year could be sitting next to an Apostle. What *does* make a difference is that everyone in the temple has attested to the same level of worthiness. Two priesthood leaders—a member of a bishopric and a member of a stake presidency—have certified by interview and signature that a person is worthy to be in the temple. The person also ratifies his or her recommendation of worthiness by signing his or her own name to the recommend.

In the temple, a person's sense of fashion doesn't matter. Everyone is expected to come to the temple clean and well groomed, and everyone dresses in similar, simple white clothing, according to the Lord's style. The only jewelry to be worn is a watch and a wedding ring, and women may wear a pair of small, simple earrings. The temple is a place of dignity and decorum, purity, quiet, beauty, simplicity, learning, and revelation. It's a place where patrons and ordinance workers say almost nothing in conversation.

So the temple is the great leveler, as stated in 2 Nephi 26:33: "and he inviteth them all to come unto him and partake of his goodness; and he denieth none that come unto him, black and white, bond and free, male and female; and he remembereth the heathen; and all are alike unto God, both Jew and Gentile."

A sister—let's call her Jane—had a weekly habit of going to an early-morning endowment session in the Salt Lake Temple. On one particular morning, there were eight men and twelve women. Jane was sitting where she could see all the men's faces. She wondered what kind of men they were. If there were a doctor or construction worker amongst the group, she couldn't tell. They all looked like good Melchizedek Priesthood brethren. Just when the session was about to begin, she overheard a women in tentative English ask a worker if she could have headphones to listen in Finnish. Other than that, the session proceeded as anticipated.

After the session, as Jane sat down in the celestial room, she overheard the ordinance worker say to the Finnish sister, "Would you like to meet one of the twelve Apostles? He was in the session with us." Jane didn't know what to think. She had studied each man's face and hadn't recognized anyone of note. Then the worker introduced the Finnish sister to Elder Richard G. Scott, an Apostle (and also a nuclear scientist). Jane considered why she hadn't recognized Elder Scott and came to a conclusion. In the temple, as we draw closer to our Father in Heaven, we see others as children of God. It isn't about spectatorship or finding the celebrities in the room. It's about individual growth and progression and seeing others as God sees them.

If you ask most regular temple-goers for a list of ways the temple has changed them, they'd look at you for several seconds and say, "I can't tell you anything specific. I just know that somehow life is better." How does the temple take a cross-section of the economic, social, cultural, and educational population of the world and make each individual better? That's where revelation comes in. It's not that you go to the temple to see angels or hear heavenly voices, although there are accounts of such experiences. Rather, it's that every time you go through the temple, the ways of the Lord's house flow into the mind and heart and, without conscious awareness, improvements come. As you distill the information, the elevating process can occur as you feel His presence in His house and want to make your house and your life more like His.

The temple is a place where men and women wear white to symbolize their desire to be pure and humble before God. In this environment, where the pride of the world is minimized, where God can teach and elevate, the temple is both leveler and elevator to everyone who worthily enters its doors. "Thou hast a few names [of those] which have not defiled their garments; and they shall walk with me in white: for they are worthy. He that overcometh, the same shall be clothed in white raiment; and I will not blot out his name out of the book of life, but I will confess his name before my Father, and before his angels" (Revelation 3:4–5).

LIFE IS FOR GIVING

It's been said that it is better to give than to receive. For benevolent, Christlike people, life is for giving, not just on birthdays, anniversaries, Christmas, or to say thanks, but as a purpose for each day. There is a gift, however, that whether given or received, is so fulfilling and gratifying, so life-changing to both giver and receiver, that words are insufficient in describing it. Most giving is associated with happy times, yet this most prized gift often comes in the wake of adversity. When bad or sad things happen, we pray we can erase the pain we've caused others or the pain others have caused us. It's then that the simplistic statement "Life is for giving" needs to be changed by eliminating one space to "Life is *forgiving*."

When Nephi, his brothers, and Ishmael's family were traveling to join Lehi and Sariah in the wilderness, some of them mutinied and demanded to return to Jerusalem. Nephi warned, "If ye will return unto Jerusalem ye shall also perish." Then they became "exceedingly wroth," bound him with cords, and planned to leave him to be devoured by wild beasts. Nephi prayed to "burst [the] bands with which [he was] bound, " and the Lord loosened them. Again they tried to seize him. This time he was saved by the pleading of Ishmael's wife and one of his daughters. Finally, the rebellious realized their wickedness and asked for his forgiveness. Nephi says, "And . . . I did frankly forgive them" (see 1 Nephi 7:15–21). When bad or sad things happen to us, do we frankly forgive?

When the Church was in Far West, Missouri, a man turned against the Prophet Joseph Smith and gave false testimony against him. Soon he became painfully aware that he had betrayed God's prophet. He decided to chop cordwood as a gift for Joseph, "if, peradventure, he would forgive and permit him to return to the fold. . . . He started [traveling to where Joseph was] with a sorrowful heart and downcast look. While on the way, the Lord told Brother Joseph he was coming. The Prophet looked out the window and saw him coming up the street. As soon as he turned to open the gate, the Prophet sprang up from his chair and ran to greet him in the yard, exclaiming, 'O Brother, how glad I am to see you!' He caught him around the neck, and both wept like children" (*Encyclopedia of Joseph Smith's Teachings,* ed. Larry E. Dahl and Donald O. Cannon [Salt Lake City, UT: Bookcraft, Inc., 1997], 271). Joseph knew the Savior's words, "And whomsoever ye receive shall believe in my name; and him will I freely forgive" (Mosiah 26:22). When bad or sad things happen to us, do we freely forgive?

A man we'll call Bob came from a prominent family and thought he was destined to be rich and famous. After receiving his PhD, he obtained a high-paying job. His wife, Sue, taught high school, and with their combined salaries, they were getting rich. But Bob wanted more. He began investing in stocks. Sue felt tension rising between them as she urged caution, but Bob threw it to the wind. A year later, Bob came to her late one night and told her he had lost their savings, their home, even all the money she would earn through the rest of the school year. In the seconds it took for her to realize the predicament they were in, she happened to look at the egg timer sitting on the stove. She walked over, picked up the timer, turned it to thirty minutes, handed it to Bob, and said, "Bob, go in our bedroom and lament the situation you have put us in. Repent of your greed, and pray for forgiveness and the strength to never do it again. When the timer rings, come out and it will all be in the past. I will never mention it again." While Bob was on husband time-out, Sue prayed fervently to have the strength to actually forgive him as quickly as she said she would, and she did! When bad or sad things happen to us, can we forgive as quickly?

In this situation, Bob's greed never resurfaced, and Sue was true to her word, truly forgiving him. She never mentioned their financial reverse again and helped him work through it. In the wood-chopping story, we don't know if this man stayed true to the Prophet Joseph, but Daniel Tyler remarked, "Those who testified against [Joseph Smith] through fear subsequently returned to the Church, some of them weeping and expressing a willingness that the Lord would remove them by death if that would remove the stain they had brought upon themselves by swearing falsely to shield themselves from the threatened death if they said aught in the Prophet's favor" (*Encyclopedia,* 271). And Nephi, faithful Nephi, frankly forgave his brothers repeatedly throughout his life.

Jesus Christ, as in everything else, is our ultimate example. He said in Matthew 5:39 that we must turn the other cheek, which means we are willing to be slapped again; that we must go the second mile, which means we've already carried another's burden one mile (see Matthew 5:41); and that we must greet the prodigal son, which means we must run to those who have offended us (see Luke 15:20). To the sick man who was let down through the roof, Jesus said, "Man, thy sins are forgiven thee" (Luke 5:20). To the woman who anointed Him with alabaster, He said, "Thy sins are forgiven" (Luke 7:48).

After Enos spent the night in prayer, He said, "Enos, thy sins are forgiven thee" (Enos 1:5). To Emma Smith, who had been complaining, He said, "Thy sins are forgiven thee" (D&C 25:3). In His hour of greatest tribulation, He said of the Roman soldiers, "Father, forgive them" (Luke 23:34). He forgives frankly, freely, quickly, and repeatedly.

Along with the traditional giving and receiving of gifts for thank-yous, birthdays, anniversaries, and Christmases, please consider a daily exchange of giving and receiving—granting and accepting forgiveness. Life is about *forgiving:* "I, the Lord, will forgive whom I will forgive, but of you it is required to forgive all men" (D&C 64:10).

A GIFT THAT KEEPS ON GIVING

Giving gifts, for whatever occasion or reason, follows a principle Heavenly Father established: "What man is there of you, whom if his son ask bread, will he give him a stone? Or if he ask a fish, will he give him a serpent? If ye then, being evil, know how to give good gifts unto your children, how much more shall your Father which is in heaven give good things to them that ask him?" (Matthew 7:9–11). His ultimate gift, as you know, is His Son, and His Son's ultimate gift was His life. It's our nature; we want to give. It is also a commandment with a promise: "Give, and it shall be given unto you; good measure, pressed down, and shaken together, and running over, shall men give into your bosom" (Luke 6:38).

But in our modern world, problems with what and how to give have overshadowed the altruistic reason to give, "freely ye have received, freely give" (Matthew 10:8). Liberal return policies are such that most any gift you give can be returned for in-store credit. Wouldn't it be simpler to save time and effort and give a gift card instead? The pragmatist would say, "Yes, just give a gift card so the person can get exactly what he or she wants; better to be pleased than unpleasantly surprised." But then, if you are giving a gift card and the person you give to gives you a gift card in return, why bother giving gifts at all?

Another gift-giving issue results from modern concerns about recycling and conserving natural resources. In the past, part of the suspense and anticipation to both giver and receiver came because the gift was concealed in beautiful paper and ribbons, but in an effort to protect our environment, the tradition of wrapping gifts is waning.

Still another issue with giving gifts in our modern world is that there are so many counterfeits. You can get look-alike Rolex watches and fake designer clothing, purses, toys, and games. MADE IN _____ often signals a product of questionable quality and origins. Also, we live with nary a moment to spare. Taking time to find the "right" gift at the "right" price may seem a waste of time and energy.

So is there an inexpensive gift that won't be returned for its monetary value, that comes in its own wrapping, that is still extremely valuable? Yes, there is! It's a book that bears the compiler's name. Actually, it's sort of like an antique from the year AD 421. It comes in a nice, blue wrapping, has a place for you to write a note on the inside, thus saving the need for a card, and only costs a few dollars.

Consider giving the Book of Mormon this year to at least one person on your gift list. In 1830, when it came off the Grandin Press, there was little publicity. No publisher financed it. A friend of the translator mortgaged part of his farm to pay the cost of printing. There were no book signings, and it didn't make any bestseller lists. In fact, it could hardly be given away. Yet, the Book of Mormon is a gift that keeps on giving and giving. Millions have received this gift and believe that the Book of Mormon "is a volume of holy scripture comparable to the Bible." They believe "it is a record of God's dealings with the ancient inhabitants of the Americas and contains, as does the Bible, the fulness of the everlasting gospel" (see "Introduction," Book of Mormon). Yet billions either have never heard of the Book of Mormon or don't believe it could be the word of God.

You may have tried to give someone a copy of the Book of Mormon only to have the recipient say, "I don't know how you can believe in the Book of Mormon because the last book in the Bible clearly states, 'If any man shall add unto these things, God shall add unto him the plagues that are written in this book: And if any man shall take away from the words of the book of this prophecy, God shall take away his part out of the book of life, and out of the holy city, and from the things which are written in this book' (Revelation 22:18–19). Obviously God said there won't be any more scripture. Right?" I have had this experience and have responded powerfully with my testimony: "I know that if you read it and follow the promise at the end, you will know that the book is true." Although I knew I was giving my best, I didn't know two very persuasive facts.

The Book of Revelation is not the only book in the Bible wherein the author warns others not to add to their writings. Deuteronomy 4:2 reads, "Ye shall not add unto the word which I command you, neither shall ye diminish ought from it." In the next verse Moses warns that those who do will be destroyed. Certainly Moses was not saying there won't be more words from God, but rather he was saying, "Don't change my words." The same is true with John the Revelator, who was speaking to the scribes of his own time who were already adding, subtracting, and revising what other inspired writers of his time had written. Origen, a most distinguished early Christian scholar who died in about AD 254, wrote complainingly, "Truly in the presence of God the Father and of the son and of the Holy spirit, I adjure and beseech everyone who may either transcribe or read these books . . . take nothing away from it, and make no insertion or alteration, but that he compare his transcription with the copies from which he made it" (Bart D. Ehrman, *Lost Christianities* [New York: Oxford University Press, Inc., 2003], 103–8).

The other fact I've learned is that when the Apostle John was writing the book of Revelation, there was no New Testament. It hadn't been compiled yet, and John would have had no way of knowing that his book would be placed last in a future compilation called the New Testament.

These facts have been useful in helping me present the Book of Mormon in such a way that the gift will be accepted and hopefully read. I sometimes just ask them to read the book and to suspend judgment until after they have read it and applied Moroni's promise: "And when ye shall receive these things, I would exhort you that ye would ask God, the Eternal Father, in the name of Christ, if these things are not true; and if ye shall ask with a sincere heart, with real intent, having faith in Christ, he will manifest the truth of it unto you, by the power of the Holy Ghost" (Moroni 10:4).

The Book of Mormon is a gift that meets every criterion for gift-giving. You may even find that giving yourself the gift of its contents every year, a chapter a night, blesses you in ways you could not anticipate. Begin with the preface written by Moroni, the testimonies of three and eight witnesses, the introduction, and then, "I, Nephi, having been born of goodly parents . . ." (1 Nephi 1:1).

WHERE & WHEN DID JOSEPH SMITH LEARN CHIASMUS?

In 1964, a young missionary serving in Germany named John W. Welch met a Catholic priest who had authored a book, *The Literary Art in the Gospel of Matthew,* which demonstrated how Matthew utilizes a Hebrew form of poetry called *chiasmus.* On a preparation day some time later, Elder Welch and his companion attended a lecture by a professor who referred to this book and pointed out chiasmic passages in biblical text. For example, Matthew 10:39 reads, "He that findeth his life shall lose it: and he that loseth his life for my sake shall find it."

a. "He that findeth
b. his life
c. shall lose it: and
c.' he that loseth
b.' his life for my sake
a.' shall find it."

The pattern is like an hourglass—a-b-c-c-b-a. The most important idea, element, or purpose of the poem is mirrored in the two *c* lines. Then the ideas of lines *b* mirror one another and lines *a* mirror one another.

On August 16, 1967, Elder Welch awoke early with a thought, like a voice in his mind saying, "If [chiasmus] is evidence of Hebrew style in the Bible, it must be evidence of Hebrew style in the Book of Mormon" ("How a Missionary Found a Book of Mormon Secret," *Deseret News,* June 12, 2008). The thought then occurred to him to look for chiasmus where he and his companion had left off reading the night before—in Mosiah 5:10–12. Opening up the German edition of the Book of Mormon, he quickly saw the pattern. His excitement was so great that he woke up his companion. "There's chiasmus in the Book of Mormon!" he exclaimed.

Excited about the discovery, Elder Welch and his companion showed examples of their findings to the professor who had lectured about chiasmus, but they concealed the poetry's origin. They had a "Professor Anthon" experience. (You'll recall that Martin Harris took copies of the characters that Joseph Smith had translated to Professor Anthon.) This professor repeated Professor Anthon's mistake. He acknowledged that the examples were very good but when he discovered where they were from, he threw the missionaries out. However, being thrown out didn't deter John Welch. He continued to search for examples of chiasmus in the Book of Mormon verse by verse, chapter by chapter. Later in life he identified a lengthy and intricate chiasm in Alma 36. The verses are abridged to show the pattern.

a. My son give ear to my *words* (verse 1)
b. *Keep the commandments* and ye shall *prosper in the land* (1)
c. Do *as* I have done (2)
d. *Remember the captivity* of our fathers (2)
e. They were in *bondage* (2)
f. He surely did *deliver* them (2)
g. *Trust* in God (3)
h. Supported in *trials, troubles, and afflictions* (3)
i. Lifted up at the *last day* (3)
j. I know this not of myself but *of God* (4)
k. *Born of God* (5)
l. I sought to destroy the church (6–9)
m. My *limbs* were paralyzed (10)
n. Fear of being in the *presence of God* (14–15)
o. *Pains* of a damned soul (16)
p. *Harrowed up by the memory of sins* (17)
q. I remembered *Jesus Christ, a son of God* (17)
q.' I cried, *Jesus, son of God* (18)
p.' *Harrowed up by the memory of sins* no more (19)
o.' Joy as exceeding as was the *pain* (20)
n.' Long to be in the *presence of God* (22)
m.' My *limbs* received strength again (23)
l.' I labored to bring souls to repentance (24)
k.' *Born of God* (26)
j.' Therefore *my knowledge is of God* (26)
h.' Supported under *trials, troubles, and afflictions* (27)
g.' *Trust* in him (27)
f.' He will *deliver* me (27)
i.' and *raise me up at the last day* (28)
e.' As God brought our fathers out of *bondage* and captivity (28–29)
d.' Retain in *remembrance their captivity* (28–29)

c.' Know *as I* do know (30)

b.' *Keep the commandments* and ye shall *prosper in the land* (30)

a.' This according to his *word* (30).

(See John W. Welch, "A Masterpiece: Alma 36," *Rediscovering the Book of Mormon,* eds. John L. Sorenson and Melvin J. Thorne [Salt Lake City, UT: Deseret Book Company, and Provo, UT: Foundation for Ancient Research and Mormon Studies, 1991], 100–113.)

John Welch sums up the evidence: "For those who are inclined to think about such matters in terms of statistical probabilities, the multiple findings discussed . . . may be summarized in the form of a series of predictions: for instance, what is the likelihood of chiasms not only accidentally occurring, but also intensifying the orderly character of the text, increasing the intricate depth of the text, significantly enhancing its artistic achievement, precisely fitting natural textual units, systematically clarifying meaning and providing demonstrable keys to textual interpretation, maintaining stylistic consistency within the writings of individual authors, emerging as reworkings of earlier texts, corresponding with other dimensions of authorial intent, appearing principally in quoted original texts as opposed to abridged materials, and working even better in Hebrew than English? The probability that all these and other similar predictions would simultaneously occur becomes remotely small, lending considerable cumulative weight that corroborates the explanation of the book's origins declared by Joseph Smith and claimed by the book itself" (John W. Welch, "What Does Chiasmus in the Book of Mormon Prove?" *Book of Mormon Authorship Revisited,* ed. Noel B. Reynolds [Provo, UT: Foundation for Ancient Research and Mormon Studies, 1997], 221–22).

The fact that there is chiasmus in the Book of Mormon adds remarkable credence to its authenticity. Where and when would Joseph Smith have learned about chiasmus? Joseph's formal education was sporadic, and what little he had came in a one-room school. Emma, Joseph's wife, said he "could neither write nor dictate a coherent and well worded letter, let alone dictate a book like the Book of Mormon" (quoted in Daniel C. Peterson, "Mounting Evidence for the Book of Mormon," *Ensign,* Jan. 2000, 19). Joseph knew nothing of Hebrew, let alone Hebrew forms of poetry, but the authors of the Book of Mormon did.

So, does the discovery of an ancient form of Hebrew poetry make the Book of Mormon truer than it was before chiasmus was found in its pages? No. Millions know the Book of Mormon is true because the Spirit testifies that it is another testament of Jesus Christ, and only a fraction of those know about chiasmus. The chiasm in Alma 36 testifies of the reality of Jesus Christ. He is the focal point as Alma testifies to his son Helaman of the sweetness that is available when we are cleansed and released from sin by Jesus Christ. Alma knew the difference. He was a damned soul who was brought to repentance and made free when he called on the name of Jesus. This testimony of the cleansing power of Jesus Christ's Atonement is available to all and is the real center, evidence, purpose, and glory of the Book of Mormon. But finding an ancient Hebrew poetic style is certainly an awesome, added bonus.

SISTER SCRIPTORIANS AND HIDDEN TREASURE

For many years, Meredith and Joyce walked around the track at the nearby high school most weekday mornings. Neither remembers whose idea it was originally, but at some point they decided to memorize a scripture each week as they walked. One week Meredith would select a scripture to learn; the next week Joyce would choose one. On Mondays the chooser would bring a slip of paper with the scripture written on it. They would practice it, repeating it to each other over and over. Then, on subsequent walks during the week, they would rehearse the scripture until it was memorized. As time passed, they also reviewed the ones they'd already learned. After several years, their bishop heard of Meredith's and Joyce's accomplishment and asked them to share the scriptures they had memorized in sacrament meeting. Meredith recited one; Joyce recited another. Back and forth they went until it was time for the closing song!

Judy learned to lean on the scriptures as a child. Her mother was an inactive member of the Church, and her father was antagonistic toward every church, so Judy never attended Sunday meetings. But Judy's aunt was a ward Primary president and arranged with Judy's parents to take her to Primary each Wednesday afternoon. As Judy recalls, she was about ten when her teacher told the class to bring thiry-five cents to help pay for a copy of the New Testament. A few weeks later Judy saw a stack of black books on the table in their classroom. She said that as the teacher explained how the scriptures were God's word and more valuable than treasure and placed the New Testament in her hands, a thrill surged through her body. Judy still remembers the verses they underlined and memorized as a class and freely shares how those scriptures became precious to her.

As a child, Kathleen loved to read, but reading aloud in front of others made her very nervous. What if she didn't know a word? When she married, her husband suggested they read scriptures together each night before prayer. Kathleen agreed but asked him to do all the reading. He agreed. After a few years, he suggested she take her turn reading. He gave her two reasons. He hoped as she practiced reading aloud to him her fear and timidity would be replaced with confidence. And, he explained, listening was too passive; the Spirit is greater with the one who reads. After much coaxing, and knowing that her husband was right, she began reading aloud. In 2005, when President Gordon B. Hinckley asked all members and friends of the Church to read the Book of Mormon, she read every word out loud! Kathleen's testimony of the book increased a thousandfold as she not only read but also listened to her own voice reading the sacred words.

For an assignment in Relief Society, Margie was asked to give a five-minute talk on the Atonement of Jesus Christ based on 2 Nephi 9. She read and prayed and reread and prayed again. The concepts seemed complicated and impossible to explain in five minutes. She persevered. As she was reading the chapter again a few days later, she suddenly wondered whose words she was reading. She had assumed they were Nephi's. Weren't all the words in 1 and 2 Nephi Nephi's words? She turned back a few chapters and found in the heading to chapter six that she was actually reading the words of Jacob, Nephi's younger brother. "Oh, wow!" she said out loud and turned again to chapter nine. She felt that personal revelation had come to enlighten her understanding. *Probably everyone else in the whole Church knew this already,* she thought, but it didn't matter. She had just had her first experience realizing not only that the Holy Ghost was helping her with her assignment but, in a broader sense, that he was helping her with the scriptures in general, and that she could apply these things whenever or wherever in the scriptures she read. The fact was that without quotation marks—which aren't used in scripture—it had never occurred to her to pay attention to whose words she was reading. She looked at the page, and another idea came as she noticed that verses 8, 10, and 13 all began with the same word. She turned the page to see if there were more similar verses. Yes! Verses 17, 19, 20, and 28. She turned the page again. Her heart did a little jump because verses 39, 40, 41, 44, and 45 all began the same way. Every one of those verses begins with "O." It was, for her, another "Oh, wow!" moment. Jacob expressed his enthusiasm with the same word she had used. His zeal for Jesus Christ and His Atonement was documented in black and white. She could almost hear him say, "O the wisdom of God, his mercy and grace!" (8). "O how great the goodness of our God" (10). "O how great the plan of our God!" (13). "O how great the holiness of our God!" (20). The prophet Jacob's excitement was very much like what she was discovering and something she could share with her Relief Society sisters. She knew and later testified that the Spirit had given her these insights.

Pam studied the scriptures daily and felt hungry for them if she ever missed a day. For some time she had felt there was something about herself Heavenly

Father wasn't pleased with, something that needed improving. She felt there was a message in the scriptures that would tell her how she could improve. One day she felt prompted to let the scriptures fall open and to read where her eyes fell. She closed her eyes, turned her quad upside down and around several times so as not to influence where it would fall open, and opened her eyes. She was disappointed because the book fell open to the Topical Guide. *Don't despair,* she thought. *Read the first word you see.* That word was *actions,* and only one scripture was listed below it: 1 Samuel 2:3. She turned to 1 Samuel and read, "Talk no more so exceeding proudly; let not arrogancy come out of your mouth: for the Lord is a God of knowledge, and by him actions are weighed." She had her message! She knew how she could improve. She had just received personal revelation.

I've often wondered what the Lord's words to those who keep the Word of Wisdom mean: "And all saints who remember to keep and do these sayings . . . shall find wisdom and great treasures of knowledge, even hidden treasures" (D&C 89:18–19). Where do we find wisdom? Where do we find treasures of knowledge? Have you ever found a hidden treasure? Is it found in the temple? Is it revealed through living prophets? Is it the Book of Mormon because it was buried in the ground as treasure is? The answer is *yes* to all of these questions. We are most blessed as a Church to enjoy treasures of knowledge in the temple, through latter-day prophets, and in the scriptures. But a few weeks ago, I gained a greater testimony of this promise because I found hidden treasure.

I had wanted to read the book of Ezekiel in the Old Testament; don't ask me why, because Ezekiel isn't your easiest read, and it took me about two weeks to finish it. There are some amazing chapters, but from chapter forty to the end, it's really tedious. An angel with a measuring stick comes and takes Ezekiel around and through a future temple, measuring everything as he goes—listing the measurements of everything he measures. Did I mention that it's really tedious? Nonetheless, I felt determined to finish it all. Then, in chapter 48, I read which tribe of Israel inherits which piece of land and which gate will be named for which tribe that will surround the future city where Jesus Christ will administer as He rules and reigns following His Second Coming. I knew the city was Jerusalem, but it never occurred to me that after reading seventy-two pages, the last verse would tell me another name for this great city and would be a touching discovery for me. The last fifteen words of Ezekiel read, "And the name of the city from that day shall be, The Lord is there." Those words filled me with joy, and I knew they were true! Jesus is coming, and the name of His city tells me where He will be! This treasure had been hidden from me.

No matter what is going on in your life, find time for the scriptures each day. Search them, memorize them, study them, find answers in them, use them, share them, teach them, read them silently and aloud, and treasure the treasures you find in them.

If you are interested in a scripture study guide, you might want to try the seminary scripture mastery list. There are one hundred scriptures, twenty-five from each of the standard works. You can get them online at lds.org.

THE HIGH PRICE OF IRREVERENCE

Angie, a young mother, received a ticket to the general Relief Society meeting in September 2007. She had recently moved to the Salt Lake area and had never been in the Conference Center. For weeks preceding the meeting, her heart skipped a beat every time she thought of being in the Conference Center and experiencing the proceedings live. She hoped President Gordon B. Hinckley would be there.

The day finally came. She arrived early, went through security, and looked around in awe. After she was politely helped to a seat, she sat pondering the beauty and expanse of the building. As the seats began to fill around her, she became increasingly aware that not everyone shared her reverential anticipation. A group of five mothers, or perhaps Young Women leaders, and nine teenage girls took their seats in the three rows in front of her. As they were getting settled, one of the mothers (leaders) took out a large bag of trail mix and passed it around, along with several water bottles. *I don't think food is allowed in the Conference Center,* Angie thought. Soon their chatter and laughter blended with thousands and thousands of women in what Angie felt was a din of disorder.

Angie had watched many general conferences that were broadcast to her stake center and knew that if the prophet were there, everyone would stand as he entered. She wondered if anyone was even watching for him. Just then, the 21,000 women stopped talking and stood quietly as President Gordon B. Hinckley walked to his seat. Tears filled her eyes as she saw the prophet of the Lord. She tried to record the scene in her mind to capture the feeling of being in the same room with *the prophet!* President Hinckley then motioned for the sisters to take their seats, and, to Angie's dismay, within one minute after being seated, the noise gradually returned to its former level.

From the minute the meeting began to the last amen, the adult and teenage sisters in front of her wrote notes and drew pictures, passing them up and down and over the rows. Angie wondered why they had come and felt disappointed at their lack of reverence. She recalled a talk by Elder Boyd K. Packer and thought they might be paying a high price by their irreverence. He had said, "When we meet to learn the doctrines of the gospel, it should be in a spirit of reverence. It is about *reverence* and how it relates to *revelation* that I wish to speak. Inspiration comes more easily in peaceful settings. Such words as *quiet, still, peaceable, Comforter* abound in the scriptures: 'Be *still,* and know that I am God.' (Ps. 46:10; italics added.) And the promise, 'You shall receive my Spirit, the Holy Ghost, even the Comforter, which shall teach you the *peaceable* things of the kingdom.' (D&C 36:2; italics added.) . . . Helaman said of that voice of revelation, 'It was not a voice of thunder, neither was it a voice of a great tumultuous noise, but behold, it was a still voice of perfect mildness, as if it had been a whisper, and it did pierce even to the very soul' (Hel. 5:30). . . . For the past several years we have watched patterns of reverence and irreverence in the Church. While many are to be highly commended, we are drifting. We have reason to be deeply concerned" (Boyd K. Packer, "Reverence Invites Revelation," *Ensign,* Nov. 1991, 21).

A couple of weeks after the general Relief Society meeting, President Packer was the visiting General Authority at Angie's stake conference. The theme was reverence. He asked the stake president to ask the members of the stake to come early and not to talk once they were in the chapel. Fifteen minutes before the meeting was to begin, the chapel and overflow were filled, and there was *no talking.* A beautiful spirit hovered over the congregation as they listened in silence to the organist playing beautiful hymn arrangements. Angie contrasted the feelings she'd felt in the Conference Center with the peace she was experiencing. During the meeting President Packer confirmed this thought as he said, "Irreverence blocks the Spirit. When you aren't reverent, you never know what you miss."

Another couple of months passed. It was the first day of 2008, and Angie was making a list of resolutions in her journal. Suddenly an idea came: "You only need one resolution this year—be more reverent. Let reverence pervade everything you do, and the Spirit will attend and bless you as never before." She closed her eyes and felt the warmth of an idea that was not her own. *Oh,* she thought, a little surprised. *There must be more to reverence than I've been thinking. Besides in the chapel, about what else am I to be reverent?* The thoughts poured in—revere God the Eternal Father, Jesus Christ, the Holy Ghost, Joseph Smith, and every prophet before and since him. Revere families and the institution of marriage, the earth and all its wonders, and the miraculous human body. Revere everything virtuous, lovely, of good report, and praiseworthy.

Reverence is so much more than being quiet during the sacrament or in the temple. Reverence is both shown in the outward appearance and felt in the heart and mind. Reverence is like a covenant. Our part of the bargain is to learn reverence and become reverent, and Heavenly Father in turn will give us revelation. So what is the high price of irreverence? Less revelation! It's this simple—live with an attitude of reverence, and personal revelation will follow.

DO YOU HAVE PIONEER COURAGE?

Every July 24, members of the Church remember and celebrate the courage of the pioneers. Setting aside a day to honor our forebears' sacrifice, service, commitment, and determination, as Abraham Lincoln would say, "is altogether fitting and proper." Though none of us—we hope—will be driven from our homes by mobs or have to blaze through an unknown wilderness, we will have numerous chances to forge a path away from and stand resolute against the evils that surround us. Pioneer-type courage is necessary in every generation.

It's springtime in Nauvoo, Illinois, in 1844. William Law, who had once been second counselor to Joseph Smith, is organizing a group to plot to kill Joseph. William invites men he believes have similar feelings to a meeting, including two nineteen-year-olds, Dennison Harris and Robert Scott. Dennison's father, Emer, is also invited. Emer is faithful to the Prophet and tells Joseph about the planned meeting at William Law's home. The Prophet tells Emer not to go to the meeting but asks Dennison and Scott to attend and report back. At the meeting, Dennison and Robert hear Joseph Smith denounced as a fallen prophet and that the group's purpose is to destroy him. When they report back to the Prophet, Dennison and Robert are asked to go to the next meeting, where they learn more of the plot. Again, they report what they heard to the Prophet. Again, Joseph asks them to attend the third meeting, saying, "'Be careful to remain silent and not to make any covenants or promises with them,' . . . He also cautioned them on the great danger of their mission" (Dallin H. Oaks, "Priesthood Blessings," *Ensign,* May 1987, 36).

At the third meeting, everyone is told they must sign an oath of secrecy. Dennison and Robert refuse. The men try to force Dennison and Robert to sign. They stay resolute. The men threaten to kill them, draw their knives, and force them into the basement. Then some of the men realize the boys' parents probably know where they are and will know where to start looking if they don't come home. Instead of killing them, they threaten Dennison and Robert that if they tell anyone about the meeting or the plot, they will be killed. Yet the boys honor their promise to Joseph and courageously report back to him. Joseph tells the boys never to tell anyone, not even their fathers, about this experience for at least twenty years. On June 27, 1844, just a few months later, Joseph Smith is killed at Carthage Jail by a mob of about 125 men who disguise themselves by painting their faces black. Thirty-seven years later, when Dennison was a bishop in southern Utah, he finally told this experience to a member of the First Presidency who was visiting his ward. Dennison had obeyed the Prophet's instructions seventeen years longer than he had been told to!

Emer and Parna Harris, Dennison's father and stepmother, had their own opportunities to demonstrate courage. Emer served multiple missions, designed and built the window sashes in the Kirtland Temple, and designed and helped build the circular staircase in the Nauvoo Temple. All the while, Parna kept everything else going at great sacrifice. A Hancock County tax assessment record shows Emer and Parna's net worth: Cattle—$50; horses—none; wagons—$50; clocks—none; watches—none; money loaned—none; stock in trade—none; other personal property—$30. Their assets totaled $130.

While members of the Church were being driven out of Missouri, mobs were detaining individuals and searching for copies of the Book of Mormon. When one was found, the owner was tied to a tree, whipped, and the book burned. Emer and Parna were determined to save some copies of the Book of Mormon. Emer created a false bottom in an old chest, placed as many copies as would fit, filled the chest with their meager belongings, and then proceeded on their journey. Parna was walking in the lead when she was met by a mob of about 400 men on horseback. The captain said to her, "Madam, are you a Mormon?" She answered, "Yes, and I thank God for it." The captain said, "We will have to search your wagon." She replied, "You have driven us around so much I think you will find nothing but rags." In searching the chest, the mob miraculously missed the false bottom and left the books undisturbed (see Kate B. Carter, *Our Pioneer Heritage* [Salt Lake City, UT: Daughters of Utah Pioneers, 1976], 19:452).

Joseph Smith exemplified courage as he survived being tarred and feathered, poisoned, falsely accused, jailed, betrayed by friends, and attacked by enemies. Yet he said, "Brethren, shall we not go on in so great a cause? Go forward and not backward. Courage, brethren; and on, on to the victory! Let your hearts rejoice, and be exceedingly glad" (D&C 128:22).

Vilate Raile understood pioneer courage when she wrote for the centennial celebration of the pioneers' entering the valley in 1947:

They cut desire into short lengths
And fed it to the hungry fires of courage.

Long after—when the flames had died—
Molten Gold gleamed in the ashes.

They gathered it into bruised palms
And handed it to their children
And their children's children. Forever.

Pioneer courage is not only something of past decades. Every day, in countries around the world, the Lord is gathering his sheep "one of a city, and two of
a family . . . will [I] bring you to Zion"(Jeremiah 3:14). Recently, five adults,
each with camera in hand, came into the Church History Museum where I
serve, clicking photos of every Church history artifact in sight. Although they
were speaking Portuguese, I could understand their excitement. After a few
minutes, one of them spoke to me in quite good English. "We are from Brazil.
To be here in Salt Lake is the thrill of our lives. When we joined the Church in
1975, we only knew two other families in our state who were members. Now
we have a mission in our city and a temple close by."

Though no mobs threaten to kill our prophet and no governor has issued
an extermination order, our courage is tested daily as we are under siege "in
consequence of evils and designs which do and will exist in the hearts of
conspiring men in the last days" (D&C 89:4). Never in history has the enemy
assailed us as now; his tactics are more subtle and more deadly. The early Latter-
day Saint pioneers struggled against physical violence that put their lives at risk;
we, the Latter-day Saint pioneers of 2009, struggle against moral violence that
put our eternal souls in peril. Pioneer courage is a trait of faithful Latter-day
Saints in every dispensation.

THAT'S WHAT I GET PAID THE BIG BUCKS TO DO

One of the hallmarks of The Church of Jesus Christ of Latter-day Saints is that there is no paid ministry. In 2002 President Gordon B. Hinckley said, "I need not tell you that we have become a very large and complex Church. Our program is so vast and our reach is so extensive that it is difficult to comprehend. We are a Church of lay leadership. What a remarkable and wonderful thing that is. It must ever remain so" ("To Men of the Priesthood," *Liahona,* Nov. 2002, 56–59). He continued by describing the demands of some of the Church assignments. But, no matter how demanding, we do what we are called to do. We are a Church of volunteers!

Sometimes, in the Church History Museum where I serve as a docent, I tell visitors who have questions that I get paid big bucks to answer their questions. They laugh when they notice that my name badge says, "Museum Volunteer." Some quick-witted visitors have quipped back, "Yeah, I know all about that heavenly pay!"

One day I was reading in the Book of Mormon, Mosiah 18:26, and discovered that we do get specific rewards for our labors in the Lord's Church. We do get paid. "And the priests were not to depend upon the people for their support; *but for their labor they were to receive the grace of God,* that they might wax strong in the Spirit, having the knowledge of God, that they might teach with power and authority from God" (emphasis added). When we are set apart for a calling and labor to fulfill our assignment, we receive "the grace of God," which helps us "wax strong in the Spirit, [have] the knowledge of God . . . [and] teach with power and authority from God."

A friend and her husband recently returned from a mission where the Church is in its infancy. They explained that most members in this country were converted within the last few years and are the first generation in their families to join. One recent convert is the gospel doctrine teacher. My friend, describing his inspiring lessons, used words such as "strong spirit," "great knowledge," and "teaches with power." It seemed impossible to her that he could understand the gospel on such an advanced level when he had been a member of the Church for such a short period of time.

To me, this gospel doctrine teacher embodies an amazing aspect about the "grace of God." It allows us to do more and to do it better than we otherwise could do. At times I've been astounded at words that have appeared on my computer screen or words that I've said, especially in conversations with people who are investigating the Church. The Bible Dictionary confirms this phenomenon: "It is likewise through the grace of the Lord that individuals, through faith in the atonement of Jesus Christ and repentance of their sins, receive strength and assistance to do good works that they otherwise would not be able to maintain if left to their own means" (Bible Dictionary, "Grace," 697). I affirm this to be true. My friend saw it in her new-member teacher; I've seen it in myself.

I grew up in a nice home with wonderful parents and siblings, but our home was in an older part of town, and somehow I thought that only rich and famous people could do important things in life. As opportunities and assignments have come to me, I've said in my head, "How could this happen? I'm just a little girl from Fifth East." Specifically, I recall these feelings when Richard and I moved to San Jose, California. I was twenty-five and had two very young children. When our bishop called me to be a Relief Society teacher, I wondered at his inspiration because there were so many older, wiser, and more wealthy women with stronger testimonies and more life experiences than me.

The Apostle Paul had these same feelings: "Whereof I was made a minister. . . . Unto me, who am less than the least of all saints . . ." (Ephesians 3:7–8). But Paul acknowledges how he was able to minister despite his weaknesses: "According to the gift of the grace of God given unto me by the effectual working of his power" (ibid.).

This is the great and specific blessing of accepting callings. We are literally and profoundly given the grace of God to do His work. When Richard and I were living in England, we met a convert family the first time they came to Church. As I was being introduced, I couldn't help but notice that the accent of the wife and mother was like that of Eliza Doolittle from *My Fair Lady*. I saw her shyness and lack of social niceties. I hoped she'd feel accepted and loved. That day in sacrament meeting, she was sustained as a Primary teacher. When the Primary president went to this sister's home, gave her the Sunbeam manual, and oriented her as to how callings work in the Church, she said that she couldn't do it. The Primary president prayed fervently in her heart to know why she had changed her mind and to know what to say. Finally, the sister told the president she couldn't accept the calling because she couldn't read. So another sister was called to read the lessons to this new sister so that she could be a Primary teacher.

About twenty years later, I was walking in downtown Salt Lake City and ran into a member from our ward in England. After renewing our friendship and reminiscing for a few minutes, I began to ask about different members of the ward and finally got the courage to ask about this sister. She was currently serving as the Relief Society president! The grace of God blesses and gives us what we need to serve Him as we serve Him by serving our fellowmen. Like the Savior, we grow "in wisdom and in stature, and in favour with God and man" (Luke 2:52). We do get paid the big bucks!

YOU ARE INVITED

During the summer, it seems that every few days an invitation comes in the mail with another date to put on the calendar. The invitations are to baby and wedding showers and wedding receptions. There are even two eightieth birthday celebrations to anticipate on our calendar right now. We all like to be invited, and we all probably do our share of inviting.

Jesus, walking by the sea of Galilee, gave an invitation to "Simon called Peter, and [to] Andrew his brother, [as they were] casting a net into the sea: for they were fishers. And he saith unto them, Follow me . . ." (Matthew 4:18–19)—a simple invitation that Peter and Andrew accepted. "The day following Jesus would go forth into Galilee, and findeth Philip, and saith unto him, Follow me" (John 1:43). And Philip followed.

Then Philip invited Nathanael by saying, "We have found him, of whom Moses in the law, and the prophets, did write, Jesus of Nazareth, the son of Joseph. And Nathanael said unto him, Can there any good thing come out of Nazareth? Philip saith unto him, Come and see" (John 1:45–46). Another simple invitation, and Nathanael went and saw and followed.

A ruler who had kept all the commandments since his youth asked Jesus how he could inherit eternal life. Jesus answered by extending the same invitation to him that He had given His future Apostles: "Come, follow me" (Luke 18:22). Like invitations we receive today, there are often conditions to accepting these invitations. Many invitations are sent with the expectation of a gift in return; some require work to honor the individual through writing memories or copying photos. Many take travel, time, and money to attend. The conditions set for Peter and Andrew to accept the invitation were to leave their nets, which was no small request. They were fishermen, providing for their families with their nets. Matthew was asked to leave his seat at the receipt of customs, also abandoning his way to provide for his family (see Matthew 9:9). Jesus asked this ruler to sell "all that thou hast . . . and come, follow me"

(Luke 18:22). Was He inviting him to live the law of consecration and to become an Apostle? We will never know, because the ruler "was sad at that saying, and went away grieved: for he had great possessions" (Mark 10:22). Instead of accepting an invitation from the Savior of the World to "Come, follow me," he went away. He walked away, choosing to follow the voice that said, "Don't follow Him."

Can you imagine how Jesus feels when men and women walk away from Him? Many of us have loved ones, friends, and neighbors who have turned and walked away from the safety of the gospel net. Turning and walking away from his father was what the prodigal son did (see Luke 15:11–24). Turning away is what Cain did (see Genesis 4:8), what Laman and Lemuel did (see 1 Nephi 2:12–14), what Sherem did (see Jacob 7:7), what Amalickiah did (see Alma 47:8), and what Judas did (see Mark 14:10). Turning from Jesus Christ is called *apostasy,* which means to revolt against, to renounce, to abandon, to defect, and to tear away from a loyalty.

There are many examples in nature that show the ease with which innocents can become prey to the cunning art of the adversary and be lost. For example, consider a flock of sheep and the deceitful practices of their natural predator, the coyote. Hungry coyotes commonly use tricks and ploys to distract sheepdogs and draw them away from their protective positions over their flocks. With the sheep left unprotected the coyotes are able to draw away and separate the lambs from their mothers' sides and the safety of the fold. The innocent, helpless lambs, when taken away from the watchful eye of their guardians, are easily picked off.

A few years ago, President Gordon B. Hinckley challenged each of us to extend the invitation to "come back" to three groups: the "many young people who wander aimlessly and walk the tragic trail of drugs, gangs, immorality, and the whole brood of ills that accompany these things"; the widows "who long for friendly voices and that spirit of anxious concern which speaks of love"; and those "who were once warm in the faith, but whose faith has grown cold." He said that many in these groups "wish to come back but do not know quite how to do it" ("Reach with a Rescuing Hand," *Ensign,* Nov. 1996, 85).

The First Presidency's Christmas message in 1985 was an invitation: "We are aware of some who are inactive, of others who have become critical and are prone to find fault, and of those who have been disfellowshipped or excommunicated because of serious transgressions. To all such *we reach out in love.* . . . To those who have ceased activity and to those who have become critical, we say, 'Come back. Come back'" ("Policies and Announcements," *Ensign,* Mar. 1986, 88, emphasis added).

To those of you who have not yet been taught the gospel of Jesus Christ or have left the fold, please accept this as a personal invitation to you. We extend the same invitation Philip gave to Nathanael: "Come and see."

SABBATH KEEPERS

On July 24, 1847, Brigham Young, sick with mountain fever, lay in a wagon overlooking the valley of the Great Salt Lake. To some the valley seemed desolate and uninviting. Filled with sagebrush, bunch grass, coyotes, jackrabbits, and rattlesnakes, it could be considered depressing if compared to the lush country-side and grassy hills of Nauvoo. Now, at least 1,000 miles away from the nearest civilization to the east, crops needed to be planted and harvested in the remaining growing season, or the Saints would starve. Nevertheless, 111 days and 1,297 miles after Brigham Young's company began their exodus, an Apostle of the Lord knew "This is the right place."

The company camped for the night and awoke the next morning to the first Sabbath day in this new land. The morning was fine and pleasant. At 10 a.m. the Saints gathered to worship and heard three Apostles speak. In the after-noon the whole congregation partook of the sacrament and listened to addi-tional talks. Then President Young, who was still very weak, made a few remarks. He reminded the Saints about the importance of keeping the Sabbath day holy—in fact, he "pleaded with them not to violate the Sabbath then or in the future" (Gordon B. Hinckley, "An Ensign to the Nations," *Ensign,* Nov. 1989, 51).

Why would this little group take an entire day off for talks and for the sacrament when their lives depended on preparing for winter? Why would the prophet speak to the Saints about keeping the Sabbath day holy? It's because President Young knew that the Lord blesses those who keep His day holy. He knew that God Himself keeps the Sabbath day holy. "And the Gods . . . on the seventh time . . . would rest from all their works" (Abr. 5:3). Brigham understood: the Lord commands it.

"Remember the sabbath day, to keep it holy. Six days shalt thou labour, and do all thy work: But the seventh day is the sabbath of the LORD thy God: in it thou shalt not do any work, thou, nor thy son, nor thy daughter, thy manser-vant, nor thy maidservant, nor thy cattle, nor thy stranger that is within thy gates: For in six days the LORD made heaven and earth, the sea, and all that in them is, and rested the seventh day: wherefore the LORD blessed the sabbath day, and hallowed it" (Exodus 20:8–11).

President Young knew then, and President Thomas S. Monson knows today that the Lord expects us, His people, to attend our meetings, rest from our work, pay respect and honor to Heavenly Father, partake of the sacrament, repent, and prepare our food "with singleness of heart" (D&C 59:13). The Lord says that fasting and prayer are important aspects of Sabbath observance and that all this should be done with gratitude and with cheerful hearts. He states in summary, "And on this day thou shalt do none other thing" (D&C 59:13). The Lord is plain in His expectations.

Blessings are promised to Sabbath keepers. The Lord says, "the fulness of the earth" will be yours. He says, if you keep my day holy, you will receive the beasts of the field and the fowls of the air, fruits, vegetables, and the good things of the earth. He promises food, clothing, houses, barns, orchards, gardens, and vineyards. He says "all things which come of the earth . . . are made for the benefit and the use of man, both to please the eye and to gladden the heart." Can you think of any temporal blessing that isn't associated with keeping the Sabbath day holy? Simply, the Lord promises you everything to make your life pleasant. Then He adds that if you do these things, your reward will not only be peace in this world but also eternal life in the world to come. He emphasizes these principles by saying, "I, the Lord, have spoken it, and the Spirit beareth record" (see D&C 59:16–24).

During a family party, an aged great-grandfather asked to say a few words to his large posterity. Knowing this might be his last counsel to them, they listened attentively as he said twelve words: "The road to apostasy begins on Sunday. Keep the Sabbath day holy." He knew that the road to apostasy and the road to the celestial kingdom diverge at the fork in the road called the Sabbath day. He knew through many years of experience that true prosperity is inseparably linked to how and where you spend the Sabbath. More than anything else, he wanted his posterity to be Sabbath keepers to help keep themselves "unspotted from the world" (D&C 59:9).

President Gordon B. Hinckley expressed his concerns regarding "'our tendency to take on the ways of the world.' He . . . said, 'We don't adopt them immediately, but we slowly take them on. . . . I wish I had the power to convert this whole Church to the observance of the Sabbath. I know our people would be more richly blessed of the Lord if they would walk in faithfulness in the observance of the Sabbath'" (Heber City/Springville Regional Conference, Priesthood Leadership Meeting, May 13, 1995, quoted in Earl C. Tingey, "The Law of the Sabbath," in *Devotional and Fireside Speeches, 1994–95* [Provo, UT: Brigham Young University, 1995], 257).

Think of the Sabbath day not as a day of restrictions but as a day of opportunity, a day to receive enough physical and spiritual strength to carry you through the next six days. The Sabbath is a day to praise the Lord, show gratitude to Him, and obey Him by partaking of the sacrament in sacrament meeting. Remember Brigham Young's example on the first Sabbath day in this valley. Not even food or shelter was more pressing than keeping the Sabbath day holy. There is no one-size-fits-all list of dos and don'ts for Sabbath keeping. As you desire to make the Sabbath a holy day and not a holiday, pray for ideas that will keep you and your family unspotted from the world. The ideas will come, as will the associated blessings.

A PARABLE: "YE TOOK ME IN"

A certain Young Men president planned to travel from Wyoming to Salt Lake City with four deacons, three teachers, and five priests to visit Church headquarters, hoping to increase each young man's testimony. He wondered where they could stay for the two nights because his budget for the trip was thin. He thought of his brother, a resident of Salt Lake City. Surely his brother and his wife would take the young men in, for he had great possessions—a 6,000-square-foot, lavishly decorated home with an indoor swimming pool and racquetball court. So the Young Men president called his brother and asked if his group could stay at his home for two nights. They would arrive late each night and leave early each morning. They would eat no food while at the brother's house, and they would each bring a sleeping bag. The brother's answer was quick and to the point: "Where would we put twelve sleeping bags? I'm sorry. We don't have any room."

Then the Young Men president remembered his mission president, also a resident of Salt Lake City. The former mission president listened to the request. "Oh, if you'd only asked when we lived in our big home," said the former president. "My wife and I would have been glad to take you in, but we have just moved to a tiny condo. Twelve sleeping bags. Wow! And twelve boys! We only have one bathroom. I wish we could. I'm sorry." Just as he hung up, the Young Men president's phone rang.

"Forgive me," the brother's voice said. "I just told my wife about your request and about my answer. She said to call you right back and tell you we would be honored to have your twelve young men stay at our home. She said she'll prepare breakfast for all of you both mornings, and you can swim and play racquetball if you have time."

And Jesus answering said, "Then shall the King say unto them on his right hand, Come, ye blessed of my Father, inherit the kingdom prepared for you from the foundation of the world. . . . I was a stranger, and ye took me in. . . . Verily I say unto you, Inasmuch as ye have done it unto one of the least of these my brethren, ye have done it unto me" (Matthew 25:34–35, 40).

A group of about seventy-five women assembled in a meeting for a charitable organization. A new woman—let's call her Francis—had joined the group and was asked to introduce herself in ninety seconds or less, as every newcomer did. At a subsequent meeting a few weeks later, one of the longtime members—let's call her Margaret—said to another member, Julia, "I feel so uncomfortable with Francis in the group. She is the most prideful person I've ever met. I get a bad taste in my mouth every time I think about the arrogant way she introduced herself."

Julia was taken aback by this unkind statement and felt confused because she had experienced the opposite reaction. Julia had heard Francis say that she was a divorced mother of three, that she was looking for work, and that she had just moved to this city because she'd gotten a job house-sitting a million-dollar home. Julia said to Margaret, "What in her introduction offended you?"

"Well, you heard her say they've just moved into a million-dollar home," Margaret criticized.

"But she's just house-sitting," Julia clarified.

"No, she's not," said Margaret. "She was bragging and trying to put the rest of us down." Julia decided to rest the subject until she had checked the facts with Francis. Later, Julia said to Francis, "Tell me about your million-dollar home."

"Oh, it's beautiful. I feel like a princess, but you know I'm just house-sitting, don't you?"

"Yes, I do," said Julia. "How blessed you are."

"Thanks for your kindness to me," said Francis. "I've felt so lonely since my divorce and having to move here and not knowing anyone. . . . "

"Then shall the King say unto them on his right hand, Come, ye blessed of my Father, inherit the kingdom prepared for you from the foundation of the world. . . . I was a stranger, and ye took me in. . . . Verily I say unto you, Inasmuch as ye have done it unto one of the least of these my [sisters], ye have done it unto me" (ibid.).

Mary's son, David, was born with spina bifida. Now a teenager, his legs are in braces, and walking is difficult. He is bright, loves life, and is socially adept. Mary and her husband, Tony, have helped David through years of surgeries and therapies. They have tried not to do anything for him that he could do for himself. Childhood seemed easy for David, but the further into his teen years he went, the harder life got for him. Having spina bifida complicates so many aspects of normal teenage life. At times, parents have to step aside and hope and pray that others will fill in the gaps. When David was approaching his sixteenth birthday, Mary felt extra anxiety because she didn't know how to help him have the normal experience of a part-time job. Mary had been pleading in her personal prayers that somehow, some way, someone would give David a part-time job when he turned sixteen so that he could learn what it was like to be an employee like other boys his age did. Earning a little money would also be good and affirming. It was stake conference Sunday, and after Mary and Tony were seated, one of their little girls needed to use the restroom. As Mary walked to the back of the chapel, a man approached her. Mary knew she had seen him before, but she couldn't remember where. "Sister Wayment," he said. "My name is Thomas Issacson. I run the Silver Moccasin Restaurant over in the Westin Hills Mall."

"Oh, yes," Mary said, remembering where she knew him from. "I love the way you chop and cook the fajitas right at the tables."

"Yes, thanks," said Thomas. "I understand that your son, the one with spina bifida, will turn sixteen soon. I'd like to hire him to be a greeter at the restaurant."

"Then shall the King say unto them on his right hand, Come, ye blessed of my Father, inherit the kingdom prepared for you from the foundation of the world. . . . I was a stranger, and ye took me in. . . . Verily I say unto you, Inasmuch as ye have done it unto one of the least of these my brethren, ye have done it unto me" (ibid.).

WHY ONLY A FEW ARE CHOSEN

The scripture "For many are called, but few are chosen" (Matthew 22:14) generates questions. Why isn't everyone who is called also chosen? Doesn't everyone want to be chosen? Who chooses who gets chosen?

Two brothers, Lyman and Luke Johnson, were called to the original Quorum of the Twelve Apostles in 1835. In 1837 Lyman E. Johnson's testimony began to show signs of decay over a financial matter. A few months later Heber C. Kimball reported what Lyman said concerning his upcoming mission to England: "Brother Heber, . . . I am sorry you are going and consider you are foolish" (*Journal of Discourses*, 6:65). In 1838, Lyman was excommunicated. He later said, "I would suffer my right hand to be cut off, if I could believe it again. Then I was full of joy and gladness. My dreams were pleasant. When I awoke in the morning my spirit was cheerful. I was happy by day and by night, full of peace and joy and thanksgiving. But now it is darkness, pain, sorrow, misery in the extreme. I have never since seen a happy moment" (Brigham Young, *Journal of Discourses,* 19:41).

Luke's spiritual resolve also suffered due to the same financial situation as Lyman's. Looking back later he said, "'My mind became darkened, and I was left to pursue my own course. I lost the Spirit of God, and neglected my duty; the consequence was, that at a Conference held in Kirtland, September 3, 1837, . . . I was cut off from the Church.' . . . By December 1837 he joined apostates in publicly denouncing the Church. Luke was excommunicated for apostasy" in 1838. In 1846, he and his family returned to the fellowship of the Saints. He was rebaptized in March 1846, came west with the original company of pioneers in 1847, and died in full fellowship at the age of fifty-four (see Susan Easton Black, *Who's Who in the Doctrine and Covenants* [Salt Lake City, UT: Bookcraft, Inc., 1997], 156–57).

Another interesting contrast is found in the lives of two men, both with the initials W.W.—William Weeks and Wilford Woodruff. William Weeks was hired by Joseph Smith as architect of the Nauvoo Temple. Joseph recorded in his journal: "I instructed him in relation to the circular windows designed to light the offices in the dead work of the arch between stories. He said that round windows in the broad side of a building were a violation of all the known rules of architecture, and contended that they should be semicircular—that the building was too low for round windows. I told him . . . that one light at the centre of each circular window would be sufficient to light the whole room; that when the whole building was thus illuminated, the effect would be remarkably grand. 'I wish you to carry out *my* designs. I have seen in vision the splendid appearance of that building illuminated, and will have it built according to the pattern shown me'" (*History of the Church*, 6:196). Thomas Bullock's journal entry of July 8, 1848, from the Salt Lake Valley tells of William Weeks's final decision about building the Lord's temples: "There was an architect in that first company, William Weeks, who had designed the Nauvoo temple. But the hopeless desolation was too much for him. [In the spring of] 1848, Brother Weeks left [the valley], saying, 'They will never build the [Salt Lake] temple without me'" (Boyd K. Packer, "The Temple, the Priesthood," *Ensign,* May 1993, 18).

Wilford Woodruff endured the same, if not more, desolation and privation, but did not lose his testimony of the restored gospel and of Joseph Smith. He said, "I am the only man now living in the flesh who heard that testimony from his [Joseph Smith's] mouth, and I know it was true by the power of God manifest to him. At that meeting he stood on his feet for about three hours and taught us the things of the kingdom. His face was as clear as amber, and he was covered with a power that I have never seen in any man in the flesh before. . . . This is my testimony, spoken by myself into a talking machine on this the nineteenth day of March, 1897, in the ninety-first year of my age" (you can read Wilford Woodruff's testimony at http://byustudies.byu.edu./dailypdfs/WilfordWoodruffStatement.pdf).

What was the difference between the Johnson brothers? It ultimately comes down to this: one followed the prophet, one didn't. What was the difference in the two W.W.s? One followed, one didn't. President James E. Faust said, "Since the beginning of the world, history has recorded many examples of those who have not been in harmony with the prophets. . . . My counsel to the members of the Church is to support the President of the Church, the First Presidency, Quorum of the Twelve, and other General Authorities with our whole hearts and souls. If we do, we will be in a safe harbor" (James E. Faust, "Called and Chosen," *Ensign,* Nov. 2005, 53).

If you've always read, "Many are called, but few are chosen" as if God calls and then chooses, here's the truth: After we are *called* by God, we use our agency to *choose* whether or not to answer His call. We refuse the call through sin and by turning away from the prophets. It's like caller ID. The phone rings and you look at the ID to see who is calling. If it's someone you want to talk to, you answer; if not, you turn away. God chooses to call you; *choosing* to answer Him makes you *chosen,* and it seems only a few do choose Him. Hence, *many* are called but *few* are chosen. The prophet Joshua said it simply: "Choose you this day whom ye will serve; . . . as for me and my house, we will serve the Lord" (Joshua 24:15). If we do like Joshua, you and I will be chosen!

WAR'S LESSONS

Every time I get to the Book of Mormon's war chapters in Alma, I feel like skipping ahead. Oh, you're right, that won't help. More war awaits me in Ether and Mormon as two formerly great civilizations annihilate themselves. So much war! Is there a purpose for recording so much bloodshed? Are the war chapters some kind of instruction manual for us in these latter days?

The depravity of the villainous Amalickiah makes for especially unpleasant reading. He is a villain's villain. He's the Nephite traitor whom we meet in Alma 46, and we learn of his death five chapters later. Prior to his death, he revolts against Helaman because he wants to become king; he leads Church members astray by flattery; he stirs up the Lamanites' hatred of the Nephites; he patiently seeks to overthrow Lehonti, the Lamanite king, using trickery and lures; he conspires with and poisons Lehonti and becomes commander of the Lamanites. Then he has his hit men kill the new king, lies to and marries the king's wife, and incites the Lamanites to battle against the Nephites. He appoints his friends as captains, does not go to battle himself, and is enraged when his army is defeated. Assuming command of the army, he successfully takes several cities and finally is slain. Not a nice guy. He is the stuff war is made of, and we could name others like him. Two chapters later, we are introduced to two thousand young men who are as righteous as Amalickiah is evil.

The people of Ammon, Lamanite converts who buried their weapons of war for peace, consider unearthing their weapons when they see the Nephites struggling to protect them. Ammon, who taught them the gospel, fears that if they break their covenant they will come under eternal condemnation. Then their sons, who hadn't made the covenant because they were too young at the time, volunteer to join the army, and Helaman becomes their leader. Entering the arena of war, these young men are tested in battle and fight vigorously in deadly combat. When the battle ends, Helaman fears that many of his men have been killed: "And now it came to pass that when [the Lamanites] had surrendered themselves up unto us, behold, I numbered those young men who had fought with me, fearing lest there were many of them slain. But behold, to my great joy, there had not one soul of them fallen to the earth" (Alma 56:55–56). Can you imagine Helaman's joy when he counted 1,999 and then saw one more? All of his two thousand sons, as he called them, were alive! *War's lesson: Evil exists and you may be called upon to help defeat it.*

Soon, sixty additional volunteers join Helaman's army and another battle ensues: "And as the remainder of our army were about to give way before the Lamanites, behold, those two thousand and sixty were firm and undaunted. . . . And it came to pass that after the Lamanites had fled, I immediately gave orders that my men who had been wounded should be taken from among the dead, and caused that their wounds should be dressed. And it came to pass that there were two hundred, out of my two thousand and sixty, who had fainted because of the loss of blood; nevertheless, according to the goodness of God, and to our great astonishment, and also the joy of our whole army, there was not one soul of them who did perish; yea, and neither was there one soul among them who had not received many wounds. And now, their preservation was astonishing to our whole army, yea, that they should be spared while there was a thousand of our brethren who were slain. And we do justly ascribe it to the miraculous power of God" (Alma 57:20–26). *War's lesson: You may be wounded even though a miracle is in process.*

Let's fast forward to Christmas Day, 1776. General George Washington's Continental Army is losing the war for American independence. The army has decreased by 90 percent since the war began, the weather is harsh, morale is low, and desertions abound. The British, with their hired Germans (Hessians), are advancing with their greatly superior numbers, training, equipment, and provisions. The Americans have been forced out of New York and have retreated into New Jersey. Even Washington expresses doubts in a letter to his brother: "I think the game is pretty near up" (Richard M. Ketchum, *The Winter Soldiers: The Battles for Trenton and Princeton* [New York: Henry Holt and Company, Inc., 1973], 243).

Stationed at the small town of Trenton in western New Jersey are about 1,400 Hessian soldiers, who feel confident that the Americans are in no condition to attack and, even if they are, the Delaware River is between them. Every night Hessian patrols traverse the frozen ground just to make sure the Americans aren't attempting to cross. But because of worsening weather and because it is Christmas Day and liquor plentiful, no patrol is sent out on the night of December 25. General Washington knows how critical his situation is and develops a plan to cross the river under the cover of a dense fog that has rolled in, which will help muffle sound and obscure vision. The motto on the lips of these patriots, some of whom have rags instead of boots on their feet, is "victory or death." As the night progresses, there are numerous setbacks, yet

Washington keeps moving forward, determined to take Trenton. Despite rain, sleet, snow, wet gunpowder, and no sleep, history books relate the miraculous victory that begins at about eight o'clock on the morning of December 26. Movies and paintings celebrate Washington crossing the Delaware. The brilliance of his stratagem changes the course and outcome of the war. Like Helaman, when the fighting is over, General Washington begins to count the toll. The final numbers showed more than 1,000 Hessian troops killed, wounded, or taken prisoner, while only four Americans have been wounded (note the similarities to Helaman's stripling warriors). *War's lesson: Even things that can seem to be negatives—desertions, fierce winter weather, fatigue—can all be the elements of a miracle.*

All bad things in life are war on some level. The prophesied "wars and rumors of wars" of the last days are in divorces, custody battles, addictions raging against conscience, private skirmishes against temptation, robberies, abuses, murders, marital wars, sibling wars, parent and child wars, neighbor-to-neighbor wars, and so it goes, on and on. Oh that we would bury our weapons of war for peace and be true and courageous. *War's lesson: No matter how close the enemy is, no matter what storm is raging, no matter how exhausting the battle, we must be firm on the side of truth, freedom, and righteousness.*

When the Israelites were at war with Syria, a similar battle with lopsided forces was unfolding. Elisha, the prophet, and his servant arose "early, and [went] forth, [and] behold, an host compassed the city both with horses and chariots. And his servant said unto him, Alas, my master! how shall we do? And he answered, Fear not: for they that be with us are more than they that be with them. And Elisha prayed, and said, LORD, I pray thee, open his eyes, that he may see. And the LORD opened the eyes of the young man; and he saw: and, behold, the mountain was full of horses and chariots of fire round about Elisha" (2 Kings 6:15–17). *War's lesson: Whatever evil assails, the righteous have unseen forces on their side. Fear not.*

THE CASE FOR NO LEFT TURNS

Michael Gartner, president of NBC News, wrote an essay about how he never saw his father drive a car. When his father was twenty-five, he stopped driving because he hit a horse. "So my brother and I grew up in a household without a car. The neighbors all had cars—the Kollingses next door had a green 1941 Dodge, the Van Laninghams across the street a gray 1936 Plymouth . . . but we had none." When Michael's brother, David, turned sixteen, his parents bought him a practically new car loaded with extras. Still, their father wouldn't drive, but their mother, age forty-three, decided she wanted to drive. She practiced in the cemetery. Who could she hurt there? So, "for the next 45 years . . . , until she was 90, my mother was the driver in the family. . . . [Dad] appointed himself navigator . . . [and] after he retired . . . almost always accompanied my mother whenever she drove anywhere, even if he had no reason to go along. . . .

"As I said, he was always the navigator, and once, when he was 95 and she was 88 and still driving, he said to me, 'Do you want to know the secret of a long life?' 'I guess so,' I said, knowing it probably would be something bizarre. 'No left turns,' he said. 'What?' I asked. 'No left turns,' he repeated. 'Several years ago, your mother and I read an article that said most accidents that old people are in happen when they turn left in front of oncoming traffic. As you get older your eyesight worsens, and you can lose your depth perception, it said. So your mother and I decided never again to make a left turn.' 'What?' I said again. 'No left turns,' he said. 'Think about it. Three rights are the same as a left, and that's a lot safer'" ("A Life without Left Turns," *USA Today,* 15 June, 2006).

In the *Deseret News,* July 15, 2006, an article titled "UPS Says Turning Right Saves Time, Money" read, "The package-delivery company has long encouraged its drivers to avoid left-hand turns whenever possible, because turning left in busy intersections is more dangerous, takes more time and uses more gas. Now the company has developed a 'package flow' software program that maps out routes to avoid backtracking and left-hand turns. . . . UPS, which last year drove 2 billion miles to move 14.8 million packages . . . , says all those right turns will save millions of dollars a year. In Washington, D.C., the new route planning technology trimmed 464,000 miles [and] saved more than 51,000 gallons in fuel . . . over an 18-month period."

So, what's the corresponding application to everyday life? What are the left-hand turns that can make us detour from the straight and narrow way? They can be personality weaknesses such as anger, impatience, laziness, or procrastination, taking counsel from our fears, succumbing to bad habits, and, certainly, the breaking of commandments, or sin.

When you sin you expose yourself in the same way a left-hand turn puts you at risk. The oncoming traffic can hit you with eternally negative consequences. Left turns can alter your depth perception and dull not only your physical senses but also your spiritual senses. It's not that you can't heal from sin, like accident and injury; it's not that you can't change course and get back on track; but it takes longer, is inefficient, uneconomical, and potentially salvation-threatening.

CTR rings remind us to choose the right way and trust in God. The truest certainty about life is that whether we choose right or wrong, light or darkness, discipline or gratification, the consequences cannot be avoided. The negative effects of turning left waste time and energy as we undo, make restitution, and repent. Turning right saves guilt, self-incrimination, and emotional, spiritual, and physical harm.

It takes faith and courage to choose the right way when peers and weaknesses of the flesh pressure us to follow the arrows pointing left. Temptations beckon everyone at every age. Moroni explains the serious consequence of choosing the wrong way: "The reason why [God] ceaseth to do miracles among the children of men is because that they dwindle in unbelief, and depart from the right way, and know not the God in whom they should trust" (Mormon 9:20).

As the hymn says, "Choose the right when a choice is placed before you" ("Choose the Right," *Hymns,* no. 239). Choosing the right way is the safest and happiest way. As Michael Gartner's father said, "No left turns." As Moroni, a prophet of the Lord, said, "Keep . . . in the right way" (Moroni 6:4).

HOW TO MOVE MOUNTAINS

Devotees of children's literature will recognize Arnold Lobel as the well-known author and illustrator of the popular children's book *Frog and Toad Are Friends.* One of his lesser-known books, *Ming Lo Moves the Mountain* (Greenwillow Books, 1982) is just as delightful and teaches children and adults a strategy for solving problems.

It begins, "Ming Lo and his wife lived in a house at the bottom of a large mountain. They loved their house, but they did not love the mountain." Rocks and stones fell from the mountain, putting holes in their roof. Heavy rains fell from the clouds that formed at the top of the mountain, leaking into their home through the holes the rocks made. "The rooms inside were damp and drippy." Shadows cast by the mountain engulfed the house and garden, blocking the sun from brightening their dark rooms and shining on their sickly crops and flowers. Although it doesn't say so directly, I believe that someone in the Ming Lo household suffered from SAD—seasonal affective disorder (depression due to lack of light). Finally, Ming Lo's wife pleaded, "Husband, you must move the mountain so that we may enjoy our house in peace."

I feel that same yearning. All I want in life, no matter how many rocks and stones pelt me, or how torrential the rains that swamp me or what mountain blocks my sunshine, is to feel peace. Ming Lo's wife counseled Ming Lo, "There is a wise man who lives in the village. Go and ask him [how to move the mountain]."

Ming Lo made four visits to the wise man. The first time, the not-so-wise man suggested ramming the mountain with a large log. The second time, he said to bang pots and pans with spoons and shout the mountain away. The third time, he advised baking special foods to appease the hunger of the mountain. On the fourth visit, Ming Lo cried in desperation, "Help me to move this mountain so that I may enjoy my house in peace!" It was then that the wise man instructed him to go home and "take your house apart, stick by stick." He told Ming Lo to bundle all the sticks and all their possessions, carry the bundles with him, and face the mountain. Then the wise man taught Ming Lo a dance to do with his eyes closed. He was to "step to the dance of the moving mountain," which was to "put your left foot in a place that is in back of your right foot. Then you will put your right foot in a place that is in back of your left foot." He was told to do the dance for a long time. Mr. and Mrs. Ming Lo did the dance of the moving mountain for many hours. When Ming Lo and his wife opened their eyes, lo and behold, the mountain had moved far away!

Mr. Lobel uses Mr. and Mrs. Ming Lo and the mountain to teach a problem-solving technique that is more than just closing your eyes and walking backward. In this simple children's story, hitting (ramming with a log) doesn't help. Yelling (banging pots and pans and shouting) doesn't help. Bribing (baking delicious desserts) doesn't help. The wise man finally gave Mr. and Mrs. Ming Lo a two-part solution to their problem. First, he gave them a task that required them to work, to actively *do* something about the problem. Taking your house apart stick by stick, packing up all your belongings, and carrying these for many hours while walking backward with your eyes closed is labor intensive. When the Ming Lo family blamed the mountain, nothing changed. When they talked together about how bad things were, nothing changed. When they tried hitting, yelling, and bribing, nothing changed. When they rolled up their sleeves and got to work, the desired results were achieved. Hard work works!

The second part to the wise man's advice allowed for the passage of time. It took time for Ming Lo and his wife to disassemble their house stick by stick, and more time to pack up all their belongings, and still more time to dance backward for many hours. Solving problems takes time. Time heals and is therapeutic. Time moves mountains. Work and time, time and work: two elements that help you resolve issues and sort through problems, bringing you desired peace. When rocks, stones, and storms are pelting you, remember the two secrets in the dance of the moving mountain: step to its music.

THE FACE OF A SAINT

In Utah, you are required to get a new photo on your driver's license every ten years. Recently, looking at the picture I had taken at the Division of Motor Vehicles in 1999, I recalled how embarrassed I used to be to show it to people because I looked so old. Whenever a clerk asked for my driver's license, I'd make a joke: "Something surprising happened when I renewed my license at the DMV. Just as the employee was taking the picture, someone shoved me out of the way and put an old woman in my place." Now, however, I look at that photo and think how young I looked.

I've had some experiences in the Church History Museum that teach me that it's not how old or young I look, but what spirit I carry about me that matters. The scenario goes like this: Someone who has never been to Utah before comes into the museum, and we begin talking. Within just a few minutes, the person will say something like, "I hope this doesn't offend you, but everyone I've met on Temple Square, at the Conference Center, and here at the museum are all alike. You seem alike, not in your actual features necessarily, but I feel something good and sincere and deep within each of you." On the downside, I've also had people come into the museum to take advantage of me for that very reason.

One day, I was explaining some artifacts in the museum when two women verbally accosted me. They spoke in loud voices and were extremely disrespectful of our beliefs. Moments before they began harassing me, I could not have identified them as enemies of the Church by how they looked. I remember a prophecy from Heber C. Kimball, a counselor to Brigham Young for more than twenty years. "In 1856 . . . a small group of friends convened in the house of the Lord. . . . The conversation was about the isolated condition of the Latter-day Saints. 'Yes,' said Brother Heber, 'We think we are secure here in the chambers of these everlasting hills, where we can close the doors of the canyons against mobs and persecutors, the wicked and the vile, who have always beset us with violence and robbery, but I want to say to you, my brethren, the time is coming when we will be mixed up in these now peaceful valleys to the extent that it will be difficult to tell the face of a saint from the face of an enemy against the people of God" (Claude Richards, *J. Golden Kimball: The Story of a Unique Personality* [Salt Lake City, UT: Bookcraft, Inc., 1966], 364). This is a true prophecy. I have seen it fulfilled.

Brigham Young made a similar comment: "There are but few here that actually know the face of a Saint from that of a devil. . . . and know and understand the truth from error, light from darkness, and be able to detect every deception and every deceptive character" (Remarks by President Brigham Young made in the Bowery, Great Salt Lake City, June 7, 1857). With the anti-Mormon women in the museum, I couldn't tell just by looking at them, but the minute they began to speak, the spirits they carried about themselves were revealed in their countenances, and there was no question as to whether they were angelic or devilish. "The show of their countenance doth witness against them, and doth declare their sin . . . and they cannot hide it" (2 Nephi 13:9).

Of course, it's my genetic code that determines my facial features, but it's what's inside—a testimony of Jesus Christ radiating outward—that visitors to Temple Square sense. Alma the Younger asked, have you "the image of God engraven upon your countenances?" (Alma 5:19). Whose image is Alma asking about? It's the image of Jesus Christ. Proverbs 15:13 describes it as a "cheerful countenance," and Psalms 4:6 and 89:15 speak of the light of His countenance. Doctrine and Covenants 88:58 prmoises that light to laborers in the Lord's kingdom: "And thus they all received the light of the countenance of their lord, every man in his hour, and in his time, and in his season." Imagine how wonderful it would have been to kneel in the presence of Jesus Christ, to be with the Nephites when "Jesus blessed them . . . and his countenance did smile upon them, and the light of his countenance did shine upon them, and behold they were as white as the countenance and also the garments of Jesus; and behold the whiteness thereof did exceed all the whiteness, yea, even there could be nothing upon earth so white as the whiteness thereof" (3 Nephi 19:25). Imagine how wonderful it would have been to be with John the Revelator when he was visited by the risen Lord, whose "countenance was as the sun shineth in his strength" (Revelation 1:16).

"The Happy Hypocrite," a short story written by Max Beerbohm in 1897, is about Lord George Hell, who enjoys gambling, drinking, and womanizing, until he meets a beautiful and innocent woman, Jenny Mere. He is shot with Cupid's arrow and asks Jenny to marry him. Jenny says that she will only marry a man with the face of a saint. Determined to marry her, he wanders the streets in confusion, wondering how he can win her love. As fate would have it, in the morning he finds the shop of a man who makes masks. Lord George buys the mask of a saint. When he sees Jenny again, he asks her to marry him. This time she agrees. On the marriage register, he signs his name as "George Heaven." Lord George changes his depraved life into a moral one by returning the monies he won gambling to people he cheated, and he gives the excess money to charities. He then buys a cottage to live a quiet, unassuming existence with Jenny.

George and Jenny are celebrating their first anniversary when a former acquaintance comes and wants to see George. A confrontation ensues that ends as George's mask is torn from his face. To his amazement, his face has changed to look just like the mask. The story, of course, is fiction, but this transformation actually happens as individuals conform their lives to the principles of chastity, honesty, sobriety, and integrity. The Lord promised Ezekiel, "A new heart also will I give you, and a new spirit will I put within you: and I will take away the stony heart out of your flesh, and I will give you an heart of flesh" (Ezekiel 36:26). Alma the Younger experienced this change of heart and encouraged others: "And now behold, I ask of you, my brethren of the church, have ye spiritually been born of God? Have ye received his image in your countenances? Have ye experienced this mighty change in your hearts?" (Alma 5:14).

You don't need to find a mask-maker to give you the face of a saint. You don't need to change your name from Hell to Heaven. It is a change of heart that changes our countenance and everything about us. Righteous living will soften you and fill you with a spirit that will be discernable to others and even to yourself. When you look in the mirror you will see the face of a saint—a true and faithful Latter-day Saint.

THE "CRUCIALNESS" OF CRUCIAL CONVERSATIONS

In 2003, I bought the book *Crucial Conversations* by Kerry Patterson, Joseph Grenny, Ron McMillan, Al Switzler, and Stephen R. Covey. Within a couple of days I had finished it and bought a copy for each of our eight children. (This is only the third book I've ever purchased for all eight at the same time. The other books were *Believing Christ* and *Bonds That Make Us Free.*) Recently, two of those children told me that they were rereading *Crucial Conversations,* and I decided I should review it as well. The book is subtitled "Tools for Talking When Stakes Are High." I've tried to think of conversations where stakes are not high and concluded that all conversations have the potential of turning crucial. Some of the most seemingly inconsequential conversations can lead to amazingly wonderful or amazingly horrible outcomes. The book teaches techniques for governing our tongues, which according to James 3:2, is how we become perfect: "For in many things we offend all. If any man offend not in word, the same is a perfect man, and able also to bridle the whole body."

One day my daughter Christine was leaving to go to early-morning seminary, and just as every other morning when I was up at 5:50 a.m. to say good-bye, I said, "Have a great day. I love you." This lovely teen stopped, turned to look me in the eye, and said, "I know you love me, but you love the piano players more." It wasn't that Christine didn't play piano; it was just that she didn't consider herself a star piano player, as some of her siblings did. It was a stab in my heart and a crucial moment for me to evaluate messages I was sending.

Another time I was praying and hoping and trying to say something to one of our children to encourage repentance. I'd tried explaining the consequences of actions and the power of building on testimony and basically saw no improvement. Then, one day at the end of a long one-sided conversation of please-see-where-you're-headed-and-change-course, I said, "I know you are a good person and want to do what's right." Instantly, this teen's demeanor changed. As tears started, my child said, "I thought you thought I was an awful person"—another stab in the heart that provided me with a needed course correction in my mothering. For me, mothering has been an instruction manual on the "crucialness" of crucial conversations.

Most of my crucial conversations aren't planned; they just suddenly happen. Then there are times when previous conversations or events have gone sour, and I know I have to either have a crucial conversation or stay in denial, allowing the situation to deteriorate. There are also "hot" topics that demand I face reality and talk about something very sensitive. There are times, however, when the best crucial conversation is silence. It's not denial, but rather the Spirit constraining. And sometimes I know a crucial conversation is needed, but for one reason or another, I know that I'm not supposed to be involved. In my experience, though, that's the exception rather than the rule. Usually, when I notice a problem or am led to see a problem, I'm the one to initiate a crucial conversation. Only the Holy Ghost knows which is which, and I trust Him. When I know ahead of time that a crucial conversation is needed, I try to spiritually prepare so that I can handle it well. However, even if the conversation occurs unexpectedly, I try to pray in my heart. (It's hard to pray and talk at the same time. I'm thankful Heavenly Father "knows all the . . . intents of [my] heart" [Alma 18:32].)

The Apostle Peter admonished us to become Godlike in our conversations: "Seeing then that all these things shall be dissolved, what manner of persons ought ye to be in all holy conversation and godliness" (2 Peter 3:11). And the Lord tells us to manifest "a godly walk and conversation, . . . walking in holiness before the Lord" (D&C 20:69).

I have learned from failed conversations that when issues become emotionally charged and neither person is thinking clearly or being Godlike in the conversation, the conversation and relationship can usually be salvaged by stepping back, taking a breath, and trying to see the big picture. Sometimes, in these tense moments, I've felt a prompting to express confidence that I know we can work through the situation in a mutually beneficial way. I've also learned to apologize—not for something for which I'm innocent, but for those things I've done wrong. And even when I feel I'm only a small percentage wrong, I am still at fault for something.

I've also discovered that it's pretty impossible to have a one-sided argument. If I drop out of the argument by saying I'm sorry, the climate changes. Sometimes simply making a joint rule that nothing that has already been said can be repeated helps clear away the debris. Sometimes changing the venue helps. "Let's go fix lunch and figure this out." "Let's continue our conversation on a walk." Sometimes putting time between a failed conversation and a future crucial one helps. "You know, I've got to be at Tara's soccer game in fifteen minutes, can we continue our conversation later?" Or "Let me think about that for a while. I'll call you later." One other great idea for defusing emotion is biblical. In Proverbs 15:1 Solomon wrote, "A soft answer turneth away wrath: but grievous words stir up anger."

Life is comprised of verbal exchanges that build or destroy relationships. I hope my ordinary, daily, minute-by-minute conversations improve relationships so that the number of crucial conversations will decrease. In the same breath, I hope that when a crucial conversation is necessary, I can speak as Nephi taught: "Do ye not remember that I said unto you that after ye had received the Holy Ghost ye could speak with the tongue of angels? And now, how could ye speak with the tongue of angels save it were by the Holy Ghost? Angels speak by the power of the Holy Ghost; wherefore, they speak the words of Christ" (2 Nephi 32:2–3).

EXPECT A MIRACLE SOON

At the end of a nice dinner at our favorite Chinese restaurant, I opened my fortune cookie and read, "Expect a miracle soon." Now I don't believe that fortune cookies actually foretell the future, but I do believe in miracles, and I do believe a miracle is coming soon.

Some miracles happen when you don't even know you need a miracle. My friend Julie was enjoying sacrament meeting one Sunday when one of her daughters started asking her over and over again to let her try on her wedding ring. Julie never takes off her ring and quietly tried to tell her daughter to stop talking and pay attention, but the daughter uncharacteristically kept pestering her. Finally, Julie placed her fingers on the ring to take it off only to discover that the stone all but fell out into her hand.

Some miracles occur when solutions to problems are unexpectedly conveyed through others. A friend told me about a time when her marriage was on the rocks. Trying to figure out what she should do, she prayed and fasted and attended the temple too many times to count. Deep discouragement was setting in because she couldn't seem to receive an answer as to the direction she should take. Then, within a few days, in ways she could have never anticipated, in general conversation with people who had no idea how thin was the thread on which her marriage hung, she was given the same idea three times—an idea that in time saved her marriage.

Some miracles come as unrelated people and situations are woven together for a purpose unimaginable at a precise moment in time. Robert and Jane told me about the time they were nine hundred miles east of their home, driving around a campsite looking for a place to camp for the night. They had been around once and were going around again when Jane noticed a child by the side of the road who was crying. She looked around for the parents and didn't see anyone nearby. Then she looked at the child again. "Stop, Robert!" she yelled. "I think that's your brother Harold's daughter Gracie." Robert stopped, and Jane ran to the child. Gracie was afraid at the strangers rushing to her until she saw her

Uncle Robert, who looked a lot like her father. Robert's brother, who lived seven hundred miles to the north, was at the campsite with his family. Neither family knew that the other was on vacation. Gracie's family was so busy setting up camp they hadn't even noticed that the four-year-old was missing.

Missionaries experience miracles. Ron and Hazel, a retired couple, had just arrived for their first day on the job as service missionaries at the Church History Museum in Salt Lake City. About fifteen minutes into the day, a young family came in for a tour. Ron asked where they were from. "France," said the man. Ron asked, in French, which city they were from, and the man named it.

"I lived in that city for several months in the mid-sixties," said Ron. "Do you happen to know a family by the name of Moreau?"

"Yes," said the man. "I am a Moreau. My mother's name is Adele Moreau."

Ron, hardly able to control his emotions, said, "I knew her. I baptized her son Rene." As it turns out, Ron had baptized this man's brother. When Ron got home, he found a photo of the day the brother was baptized. In the photo, Ron is holding a little boy who grew up to be the man he had met in the museum.

A full-time missionary's father told of an experience his son had. Elder Timothy was serving a mission in a large metropolitan city in California. One day he and his companion took a wrong transfer on the bus and found themselves in a part of town that concerned them. Homeless-looking people lined the streets. The missionaries were trying to find way out of the area when they noticed a man who was calling to them. They walked toward the man and began a conversation with him. The man asked Elder Timothy where he was from. He answered that he was from Utah. "Where in Utah?" he asked.

"Salt Lake City," said Elder Timothy.

"Where in Salt Lake?" the man asked.

Elder Timothy wonderingly answered, "In a small suburb called Canyon Rim."

"Is your mother's name Wendy?" the man asked. Elder Timothy was so shocked he couldn't get an answer out before the man said, "And her father's name is Earl Kennedy?"

"Yes," said Elder Timothy, completely baffled.

"I know your mother and grandparents," he said, "and lots of people in your ward. I lived next door with the Shingletons as a foster child for four years about twenty-five years ago." When this news got back to the Shingletons, they said they had been trying to reconnect with him for many years.

One of my docent friends in the museum told me about an *Ensign* article that captivated her interest for several weeks. She carried the magazine around with her, read and reread the article, told everyone who would listen about it, and was puzzled by the pull the article had on her. Then one day a visitor came into the museum who began to question her about the topic in the *Ensign* to which she had been "addicted." The visitor asked her a question the article answered. With the help of the Spirit and fluency in the topic, she was able to teach the amazed visitor. As soon as the visitor left, so did her interest in the article.

Miracles happen in callings. My friend Angela was having a bad year. She had health and work struggles, and she was also frustrated with the class she had been called to teach in Primary. She felt like she should ask to be released, something she had never done before. Meanwhile, in the bishop's office, the bishopric was kneeling in prayer, inquiring of the Lord who should be the new Primary president, and Angela's name came to the bishop. As they discussed it they knew she was the right person, but they were also aware of the current problems facing Angela and her family. After the decision was firm, the bishop prayed that Angela, through the Spirit, would be given a little advanced notice, so she wouldn't be caught completely by surprise. When Angela prayed to know if it would be appropriate to ask for a release, the thought came into her mind, "You are going to be the new Primary president." *Oh, no,* she thought. *Say it isn't so.* When the bishopric rang her doorbell a few days later, she opened the door and said, "I know why you are here."

Hopefully, you've experienced enough miracles in your life that you know you can expect another miracle soon.

TOOLS

A tool, by definition, is something that's used as a means to an end. In early Church history it is evident that certain people were raised up to perform specific tasks to accomplish and further the Restoration of the gospel of Jesus Christ. One of these men was Joseph Knight Sr., whom Joseph Smith called "Father Knight." Joseph first met Father Knight while boarding with him near the Susquehanna River in 1826. Father Knight was one of the first people to hear the Prophet's story, and he believed him. *Believing is a tool.* When Joseph and Emma went to get the plates from Moroni on the night of September 22, 1827, they used Father Knight's carriage. *A carriage is a tool.* During the translation of the Book of Mormon, ever-present economic concerns required Joseph and Oliver to stop and seek employment, but Father Knight came with food, lined paper, and money to purchase more. *Food, lined paper, and money are tools. Responding to someone in need is a tool.* When the Lord commanded the Saints to go to "the Ohio" (D&C 37:1–4) to be "endowed with power from on high" (D&C 38:32), Joseph and Emma made the arduous journey in January snows (their eighth move in four years—and Emma was six months pregnant) in Joseph Knight Sr.'s sleigh. *Helping someone fulfill a calling is a tool. Being willing to do the Lord's will is a tool. Being willing to sacrifice personal comfort is a tool.*

Martin Harris is remembered for mortgaging his farm to finance the printing of the Book of Mormon. *Taking personal risk for a righteous cause is a tool.* Martin was at the Grandin Press on March 26, 1830, when the first bound copy of the Book of Mormon came off the press. *Being present at important times is a tool.* Martin picked up that first copy and presented it to his brother Emer and signed it to him. Emer brought that first Book of Mormon with him when he came west and remained true to his testimony all of his life. *A testimony is a tool.* Emer labored as a carpenter and joiner in the Kirtland Temple, creating the window sash and other intricate details within that sacred building. He is also credited with building the winding stairway in the Nauvoo Temple. *Carpentry skills are a tool. Being willing to work hard is a tool.*

Eliza Roxey Snow started writing poetry at a young age. She won prizes and had at least twenty poems published before she joined the Church in 1853, when she was thirty-one. After joining the Church she wrote poems for important occasions. Many of her poems became hymns. In our current hymnal, she wrote the text for "Again We Meet Around the Board" (no. 186); "Great Is the Lord" (no. 77); "How Great the Wisdom and the Love" (no. 195); "In Our Lovely Deseret" (no. 307); "O My Father" (no. 292); "The Time Is Far Spent" (no. 266); "Though Deepening Trials" (no. 122); and "Truth Reflects upon Our Senses" (no. 273). *The skill to write poetry is a tool. Working hard to develop a talent is a tool.* She was the first president of the Relief Society after the Church moved west, and she served in that capacity for twenty-one years. She was commissioned by Brigham Young to organize Relief Societies throughout the Church. *Being willing to travel for a righteous cause is a tool.* She has been called the "captain of Utah's woman-host." *Talents to lead and organize are tools.*

The tools of Heber C. Kimball's trade were the anvil and hammer of a blacksmith and the wheel and kiln of a potter. He was one of the first British missionaries after Joseph heard the voice of the Spirit whisper, "Let my servant Heber go to England and proclaim my gospel." *Being worthy to accept a mission call is a tool. Serving as a missionary is a tool.* He was faithful to his testimony throughout his life and served for twenty-four years as first counselor to Brigham Young. *Willingness to serve a long time is a tool. Enduring to the end is a tool.*

Newel K. Whitney was a prosperous merchant. He organized and managed his store with precision. *Business acumen is a tool.* He taught himself to be an accountant by studying *The Scholars Arithmetic,* which was probably the how-to book on business finance of the times. *Reading, studying, and learning are tools.* He and his wife, Ann, joined The Disciples of Christ, who claimed authority from the Bible to baptize but not to confer the gift of the Holy Ghost. Newel and Ann desired this great gift, began studying the New Testament, and prayed to know how to receive the Holy Ghost. One night, a cloud of glory settled over both them and their home, and they heard a voice say, "Prepare to receive the word of the Lord, for it is coming" (Edward W. Tullidge, *Women of Mormondom* [New York: Tullidge and Crandall, 1877], 42). *Spiritually preparing yourself is a tool. Desiring spiritual gifts is a tool.* He and Ann provided housing for Joseph and Emma. They also gave Joseph the use of two rooms above their store, one to translate in and one to use as a schoolroom for the School of the Prophets. *Generosity is a tool. Seeing a need and filling it is a tool.*

Each of these early Saints and thousands more became the Lord's tools in building up His kingdom. He blessed them with differing abilities and with the necessary tools and talents to complete their responsibilities. Today, we Latter-day Saints are tools and have been blessed with differing abilities. We have the necessary tools to complete our responsibilities. He has given you many tools—more than you know. Pray to be an instrument in His hands, and with Alma you can say, "The Lord did . . . answer my prayers, and has made me an instrument in his hands" (Mosiah 23:10).

INDEX

abuse: emotional, 33; zero tolerance for, 31

acceptance, 147–49

accountability, in in-law relationships, 4

activities, over scheduling, 18

Adams, John, 12

Allen, James B., 101

Anthon, Professor, 122

appearance, 37–38, 163–65

autonomy, 38

Ayer, Eleanor H., 42

Ballard, Melvin J., 85

baptism, of Joseph Smith, Samuel Smith, and Oliver Cowdery, 23

BART, 82

beauty, 37–38

Beck, Julie B., 25–27

Beerbohm, Max, 164–65

Berlin, Irving, 85

Bible, 97

big picture, 81–83

blessings, of Church membership, 135–37

Book of Mormon: as evidence of continuing revelation, 97; as gift, 118–19; challenge to read, 126; chiasmus in, 121–24; learning from wars in, 155–57

Boss, Chester, 49

Boss, Peter, 49

boys: compared to girls, 35; ideas to help raise, 29–34

brother of Jared, 93–94

Brown, H. Jackson, Jr., 42

callings, blessings of, 135–37

cancer: author gives in spite of, 73–74; finding hope through, 77

Carnegie, Dale, 85

cell phones, 46

Chadwick, Bruce A., 38

character: discipline builds, 34; molding daughters', 37

chiasmus, 121–24

children: as reason for good in-law relationships, 5; babying, 17; enabling, 9–10; ideas to help raise, 29–39; love for, 61–63; mistakes good parents make with, 18–20; over scheduling activities for, 18; parenting pyramid for, 13–15; preparing, for missionary work, 25; teaching, about marriage, 41–43; teaching, about millennium, 57–59; teaching civility to, 45–47; teaching

patriotism to, 49–51; teaching
   sacrament to, 53–55
choices, 33
chosen, 151–53
Church of Jesus Christ of Latter-day
   Saints: blessings of membership in,
   135–37; technology for sharing,
   99–102
cinnamon rolls, 74–75
civility, 45–47
cleanliness, 26–27
Columbus, Christopher, 50
communication skills, 38–39
complaining, 69–70
confidence, for girls, 37–38
continuing revelation, 97–98
conversations, crucial, 167–69
countenance, 163–65
courage, 33, 131–33
Covey, Stephen R., 167–69
Cowdery, Oliver, 23, 86, 97
criticism, 11
Crowley, Mary C., 85
Crucial Conversations, 167–69
CTR rings, 160

daughters-in-law, 3–7
dead, vision of redemption of, 103–5
discipline, 30, 34
Doctrine and Covenants, as evidence
   of continuing revelation, 97
dolls, 18
don't, 32
dreams, expecting children to fulfill
   your, 19
driving, 46, 159–60

education, emphasizing, 37
emotional abuse, 33
emotional courage, 33
emotional stability, 38

emotional well-being, 18
enabling, 9–10
equality, 111–12
example: mothers as, 21–23, 36; of
   good marriage for children, 43
experience, 82–83
extremes, in parenting, 19

The Family: A Proclamation to the
   World, 36–37, 41, 43
father(s): choosing your children's, 36;
   importance to boys of, 30. *See also*
   parents
Faust, James E.: on importance of
   fathers, 36; on supporting prophet,
   152
fear, allowing boys to express, 31
finances, 38
"fix it" syndrome, 9–10
forgiveness, 113–15
Forni, P.M., 46
Friel, John C. and Linda D., 17
friend(s): being your child's, 18;
   giving to, 73–76
Gartner, Michael, 161
girls: compared to boys, 29; ideas to
   help raise, 35–39
giving, 73–76, 117–19
gorilla, 81–83
greed, 114
Grenny, Joseph, 167–69

"The Happy Hypocrite," 164–65
Harris, Dennison, 131–32
Harris, Emer and Parna, 131–32
Harris, Martin, 122, 175
Heavenly Father, knows our names,
   65–67
Hill, Brian J., 13–15
Hinckley, Gordon B.: attends general
   conference, 129; challenges

members to read Book of
Mormon, 126; invites people back
to church, 140; on growth of
Church, 135; on keeping Sabbath
day holy, 144; on marriage, 42; on
technological advancements, 100
Holy Ghost: scripture study and, 126;
tender mercies and, 89–91; worry
and, 86
home, tender mercies in, 90–91
homemaking, 26–27
honor, for parents and in-laws, 4
hope, 77–79
hovering, 32
husbands: cannot read minds, 10–11;
criticizing, 11; enabling, 9–10;
neglecting, 17

independence, 38
in-law relationships, 3–7
invitations, 139–41
irreverence, 129–30

Jesus Christ: accepting invitation of,
139–41; as example of forgiveness,
114–15; hope in, 78–79; knows
our names, 65–67; millennium
and, 57–59; strength through,
69–72
Johnson, Lyman and Luke, 151

Kimball, Heber C., 151, 163–64, 176
Kimball, Spencer W.: Official
Declaration received by, 97; on
marriage, 42; on millennium, 59;
on technological advancements,
100
Knight, Joseph Sr., 175

language, using clean, 46
Law, William, 131

left turns, 159–60
less, doing, 25–26
limits, 30, 31
Lincoln, Abraham, 39, 131
Lobel, Arnold, 161–62
love: for children, 61–63; for
daughters, 39; for in-laws, 3–7
Lowell, James Russell, 86

marriage: as priority, 17; finding good
father for, 36; four mistakes of
good wives in, 9–12; teaching
children about, 41–43
McMillan, Ron, 167–69
mercies, 89–91
millennium, 57–59
mind-reading, 10–11
Ming Lo Moves the Mountain, 161–62
miracles, expecting, 171–73
missionary work: preparing children
for, 25; technological
advancements and, 99–102
mistakes: of good parents, 17–20; of
good wives, 9–12
money, 38
mothers: as example for daughters,
36; as example for vocal prayers,
21–23; hovering, 32; Julie B.
Beck's counsel on, 25–27. *See also*
parents
mothers-in-law, 3–7
mountains, moving, 161–62

names, 65–67
Naomi, 93
nurturing, 26–27, 61–63

order, 26–27, 33
Origen, 118–19

Packer, Boyd K.: on reverence,

129–30; on temples, 108–9
parable, of acceptance, 147–49
parents: being unified as, 36–37;
    honoring, 4; parenting pyramid
    for, 13–15; seven worst mistakes of
    good, 17–20. *See also* father(s);
    mothers
past, digging up, 11–12
patriotism, 49–51
Patterson, Kerry, 167–69
Pearl of Great Price, as evidence of
    continuing revelation, 98
Pentateuch, 97
perception, 81–83
physical work, 31
pioneers, 131–33
plate, 74–75
praise, 33
prayer: for good in-law relationships,
    4–5; Lucy Mack Smith as example
    of, 21–23
problem solving, 161–62
promised land, 93–94
prophet, supporting, 152

Raile, Vilate, 132–33
reading, 32
relaxing, 34
Restoration, 50
revelation, continuing, 97–98
reverence, 129–30

Sabbath day, 143–45
Sachs, Jeffrey D., 101–2
sacrament, 53–55
safety, civility and, 45
sandwich, 73–74
Satan, 59
Scott, Richard G., 36, 112
Scott, Robert, 131–32
scriptures: as evidence of continuing

revelation, 97–98; studying,
    125–28
Second Coming, 57–59, 78–79
silence, John Adams on, 12
Simons, Daniel J., 81
sin, compared to left turns, 162
Smith, Dean, 86
Smith, Emma, 100, 123, 175
Smith, Hyrum, 103
Smith, Jesse, 22
Smith, Joseph: as example of
    forgiveness, 113–14; called by
    name, 65; chiasmus and, 121–24;
    courage of, 132; goes to Hill
    Cumorah, 100; hires William
    Weeks, 151–52; Joseph Knight Sr.
    helps, 175; martyrdom of, 103;
    mother's example, 21–23
Smith, Joseph F., 97, 103–5
Smith, Joseph Fielding, 100
Smith, Joseph Sr., 22
Smith, Lucy Mack, 21–23
Smith, Mary Fielding, 103
Smith, Samuel, 23
Snow, Eliza Roxey, 176
spiritual well-being, 18
spirit world, vision of, 103–5
strength, through Jesus Christ, 69–72
structure, for children, 18–19
swearing, 46
Switzler, Al, 167–69

talking: encouraging, for boys, 32; too
    much, 11–12
Taylor, John, 97
technology, 99–102
temple: equality in, 111–12;
    sacredness of, 107–9; William
    Weeks hired to build, 151–52
temple marriage, 42
tender mercies, 89–91

tools, 175–77
Top, Brent L., 38
Torah, 97
train, 82
travel, 99–102
trials: hope in, 77–78; take us to
    promised land, 93–94
Tyler, Daniel, 114

Uchtdorf, Dieter F., 70
United States, role in Restoration of,
    50

value, for daughters, 39
vision, of spirit world, 103–5

wars, 155–57
Washington, George, 12, 46–47,
    156–57
Weeks, William, 151–52
Welch, John W., 121–23
Whitney, Newel K., 176
Wilder, Laura Ingalls, 100–101
wind, 93–94
wives, four mistakes of good, 9–12
women: nurturing opportunities for,
    61–63; scripture study and,
    125–28
Woodruff, Wilford, 97, 151–52
worrying, 85–87
writing, 32

Young, Brigham: on beauty, 37–38;
    on faces of Saints, 164; on keeping
    Sabbath day holy, 143; on women
    and finances, 38; revelations of, 97

Zinsmeister, Karl, 36

ABOUT THE AUTHOR

Marilynne Todd Linford has written nine other books: *ABCs for Young LDS, I Hope They Call Me on a Mission Too!, Is Anyone Out There Building Mother's Self-Esteem?, Slim for Life, Breast Cancer—Support Group in a Book, A Woman Fulfilled, Give Mom a Standing Ovation, Sisters in Zion,* and *We Are Sisters.* She and her husband, Richard, have eight children and twenty-one grandchildren. She enjoys studying LDS Church history and serves as a docent in the Church History Museum. She serves in the Salt Lake Temple and on the Materials Evaluation Committee of the Church. Her hobbies include playing piano duets and Scrabble with anyone who is willing. For her, life's most beautiful moments include being with Richard and any combination of family at Church or national historic sites, on beaches where the air and water are the same warm temperature, or hiking the red rock canyons of Southern Utah.